Reading *Another Lau...*  ...iate my friends and family so ...iends is very evident through... ...to me that I may not be appr... ...ted the emphasis he places on enjoying the little things in life, things we often take for granted, like those long walks and sunsets John speaks of and finding laughter in the ordinary day-to-day events.

I know John well and have always appreciated his humble spirit and the ability he has to laugh at himself. His stories of some of the little blunders are so comical they made me laugh, just imagining John in those situations. What touched me the most is how highly John speaks of his wife. I too have a "Carol" in my life, and it made me want to write a tribute to the beautiful person my wife is. It made me appreciate her more.

Finally, I love how John promotes Jesus and his direction, provision, and protection throughout their life journey. The testimonies of Jesus's healing power and leading, even without us realizing it, is a fact I too have experienced. In the last chapter, he states "God is involved in our lives, whether we notice it or not. The test is to open our eyes and observe just what God is doing." All I can say is, amen to that. For some good, light-hearted reading that will leave you appreciating life much more, I would highly recommend John's book.

—Rev. H. John Klooster

Rev. H. John Klooster has been in the ministry for twenty-seven years and has pastored New Life Community Church in Edmonton, Alberta for the last eight. He has been married to his lovely wife Carol for thirty-two years and has two adopted children, Joshua, age twenty-six, and Kylie-anne, age twenty-one. They are in process of adopting a third child, Chanel, who is almost five.

John's latest book, *Another Laugh and Another Tear*, is the wonderful story of how God is faithful from the start. An overriding theme here is the love that John has experienced and expressed in his life. His family always believed in him, and John's ministry reflects this love. It is truly inspirational what God has done with John and Carole through the ups and downs of life and ministry. Sit back and enjoy the many stories John wants to share with you.

—Brian Stevenson

Brian Stevenson is retired from his career in industry. He has been involved in the local church for many years and in various capacities. He has also travelled as a short-term missionary to Africa.

If you want a glimpse into how Christian faith binds together family, friends, and ministry colleagues, you will benefit from John Telman's biography, *Another Laugh and Another Tear.* It becomes apparent to the reader that John is surrounded by a great cloud of witnesses who testify to the goodness of God and their love for all the saints. The reader can draw upon the courage of these believers, who would urge everyone to *"run with endurance the race that is set before us"* (Hebrews 12:1).

—Dr. Rob Lindemann

Dr. Rob Lindemann is the Academic Dean of Vanguard College in Edmonton, Alberta.

John Telman's book chronicles the story of a man God has chosen to be one of his teachers and leaders. The narrative weaves from an initial discussion of his godly heritage through his formal education and pastoral ministry, all the while infused with real-life humor and mirth. God's hand has been on John since his birth, and the work details the confirmation of that commission as evidenced by a life of dedication and service.

His love for his family is evident. He adores his beloved wife Carole, his partner in mission and ministry for more than thirty years. He has loved her with a warmth that glows in every line he writes about her. But John also admits his struggles and challenges. Throughout the work, he knows whom he has believed. The writing reads as coming from a man firmly planted in his faith and as one who seeks to make Christ better known.

The work is not formal or academic; appropriately, you will laugh and shed a tear. It is the telling of a man's walk with God and the telling of him literally all over the world.

Son, friend, husband, father, musician, teacher, and preacher, John is a true soldier of Jesus Christ. The book reflects this and is a highly readable account of a life well magnified in God's service. It ends with what one would expect—a call to surrender one's life to the man from Galilee, and to claim the salvation he so freely offers.

—David Stam

David Stam is a lawyer from Edmonton, Alberta.

I really don't *know* John. I really only *know of* John, by virtue of pastoring in the same province and denomination together. I mention this to say that by reading his book, I finally had the chance to get to know him! In doing so, I felt that I'd met a kindred spirit. Sharing a common Dutch heritage, being former worship ministers, and growing up in a loving, musical home established an easy common ground between us.

In picking up a copy of his book, I anticipated sitting down to read an autobiographical account of this life. I was wrong. Instead I sat down to discover stories of friends and family who had shaped his life. It's a tribute really. What a wonderful way to get to know a person! Instead of making himself the focus of his own writing, he instead shines a spotlight in the direction of the relationships that were most meaningful to him.

To me, this unique approach reflects a godly man who humbly recognizes that God oftentimes uses the people in our lives to mold, shape, and direct our steps. This book caused me to reflect upon the relationships that have guided my own personal life journey and prompted a thankfulness and respect similar to John's for those whom God has brought into my story. I hope this book might do the same for all who read this book.

—Phil Spoelstra

Phil Spoelstra has been a full-time worship leader for almost twenty-five years, most recently as the associate pastor at Broadway Church in Vancouver, British Columbia. He currently serves as the assistant superintendent of the British Columbia and Yukon District of the Pentecostal Assemblies of Canada, and lives in Langley with his wife Christine, three teenage children, and one wiener dog.

You will find this a fascinating read. It is filled stories of both struggle and triumph. It is what I call "real life." The journey of John Telman and his family, friends, and associates touches us all. In many ways it is also the story about each one of us as pilgrims of Jesus Christ on earth. You will be inspired by this wonderful legacy of an outstanding Christian family. It honors family as the fundamental building block of what is important in life. But above all, it exalts Jesus Christ as Lord of All.

—Dr. George Johnson

Dr. George Johnson is the lead pastor of Harvest City Church in Vancouver, British Columbia. He is a spiritual father and mentor to leaders both home and abroad. He has served in church ministry for more than fifty years.

In this book, John Telman reminisces of a life lived for God. This is illustrated well by a line he uses often: "a laugh and a tear." Sometimes life is hard, and sometimes life is full of joy. John and his family demonstrate the joy of the Lord, even (and maybe especially) when external circumstances seem difficult.

As a child of missions myself, I especially enjoyed the international notes in their lives, whether serving in ministry in Singapore or experiencing the dynamics of Dutch families now living in Canada. I am happy to recommend Telman's memories of his parents, wife, children, and friends to all who want to know more of what it is like to follow Christ into every situation of life.

—Dr. Daryl Climenhaga

Dr. Daryl Climenhaga teaches Global Studies (Christian missions) at Providence University College and Seminary in Manitoba. He has lived his life in three parts: one-third in Zambia and Zimbabwe, one-third in Pennsylvania and Indiana, and one-third in Manitoba.

Another Laugh and Another Tear is a terrific story of faith, hope, and love as told by a first-generation Canadian. The narrative traces the real-life journey of a family as it struggles through the challenges of living and how hope and faith win the day.

—Laurence Berteig

Laurence (Laurey) Berteig is currently the executive pastor at Westminster Chapel in Bellevue, Washington and has served in churches in Canada and the United States as a church musician, composer, conductor, and educator.

John's book, *Another Laugh Another Tear*, was a stroll down memory lane for me. I've known John Telman and the Telman family more than forty-five years. John takes readers through his life of joyful highs and crazy laughs to extreme lows and tears of despair. He also allows the reader to reflect on their own journey of laughter and tears. Life does have many moments of laughter and tears, regardless of our social standing, financial status, or family life.

As I read through the pages of John's life, I looked back with 20/20 vision and saw that, like John, God has been there for me in the laughter and walked with me through the tears. This book is a testament to the hand of God working in every area of his life, molding and shaping him to be a husband, father, and minister to the needs of others. Again, not only did I enjoy reading about John's life, but I saw the blessings I've received while reflecting on my own.

—**Curtis Walters**

Curtis Walters works in real estate investing and property management and is a licensed real estate agent in Edmonton, Alberta.

Hymnwriter Fanny Crosby proclaimed, "This is my story, this is my song. Praising my Savior all the day long." The significance of the story of our lives is rooted in our understanding of God's providence and goodness in weaving together all the parts of the journey. With color and keen insight, John Telman tells the story of growing up, education, marriage, family, and ministry—all framed with "a laugh and a tear." I suspect you will find parallels between John's story and your own. As a result, you will join John in giving praise to God for his faithfulness and guidance in every step of your earthly passage.

—**Daniel Henderson**

Daniel Henderson is an author and the president of Strategic Renewal, which provides resources for spiritual and personal renewal, equipping and mobilizing churches to pray, and training pastors to lead the Church in prayer.

Another Laugh and Another Tear is more than the continuation of the Telman story. It is the continuation of the story of the kingdom of God. I am reminded of Luke's words in Acts 28:30–31. We want to hear of Paul face to face with Ceasar, but instead we're left with the open door of kingdom work. The Telman family has walked through that open door and has been faithful witness to the kingdom of God in Christ Jesus. It was a joy and pain to read of the laughs and tears experienced by this family. As I read it, I found myself saying, "That's the Telmans I remember" and "That's the God I know."

All along the journey of life, John has gained nuggets of truth that he shares with his readers in an open and honest way. Thank you for sharing the continuation of the story. I found it to be *Tov meod*—in Hebrew, "very good," "very functional," or "very useful." It's the story of the extraordinary kingdom of God expanding through ordinary people in ordinary life settings.

—Dr. Roc Weigl

Dr. Roc Weigl has been the senior pastor of Stony Plain Baptist Church for the past thirty years.

Pastor John Telman details an affectionate story of love, life, legacy, and music. *Another Laugh and Another Tear* is a masterful memoir that captivates the soul and reminds us all that we are our Father's adored creation. Through joy and pain, we are truly more than conquers in Jesus Christ. For those who love stories about music, or for those who are just lovers of a true love story, this is a must read.

—Dr. Crystal Lumpkins

Crystal Lumpkins, PhD, is a devoted Christian wife, mother of three, public health communication scholar, and faculty member in the greater Kansas City area. She also is an aficionado of praise and worship music and sings with her church praise team, choir, and sister on special occasions.

I have known John Telman since 1997, when I had the privilege of performing with his Jesus Jazz Band at Sheffield Assembly of God in Kansas City. This book is a wonderfully inspirational reflection on his life (so far!) and mirrors both his wonderful spirit and commitment to serving God through his ministry and life. You will find, as I did, that you will always want to read just one more page… then another… until you run out of pages.

—Dr. Chris Waage

Dr. Chris Waage is a professional bass trombonist and educator based in the Kansas City metro area. Raised in Temple, Texas, he has been active as a performer, conductor, clinician, and private instructor since 1982.

What a great read. I've worked with John for years writing musical arrangements and even helping out in Singapore, but I didn't know John's backstory. I love the way he's honored God by honoring the people in his life. Great job, John. I love how you are running the race with love and perseverance. Dear reader, this book will help you discover the power of family and music, and the joy and challenges of following God with your whole heart.

—**Mark Cole**

Mark Cole is a follower of Jesus, founding arranger of Praisecharts.com, and music pastor of more than thirty years. He's a travelling musician, having visited sixty-five countries, and a writer and teacher.

My relationship with John Telman and his wife Carole dates back to my early days of ministry in the Western Ontario District of the Pentecostal Assemblies of Canada. We share the memory of being ordained on the same day and sitting beside each other during the ordination service.

It has been a pleasure to get reacquainted with these friends over the last couple of years as we have both transitioned to ministry in the United States with the Assemblies of God.

Another Laugh and Another Tear gave me an insight and understanding of John and his family. John has the ability to tell stories of his upbringing in such a way that brings the reader right into the experience. His use of humour adds to the flow of the narrative, even when describing difficult seasons and events. The way in which John honours every person in his story is commendable, especially in a time when honour is being silenced in the wake of criticism.

I would encourage you to take a few hours to dig into this book… I'm sure it will inspire another laugh and another tear.

—**Dr. Jamie Stewart**
Lead Pastor, Life Church, Kissimmee, FL

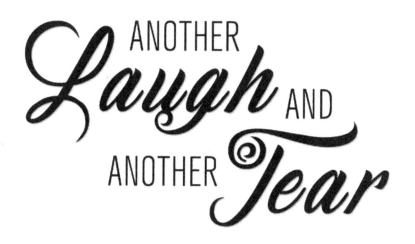

ANOTHER *Laugh* AND ANOTHER *Tear*

John W. Telman

Printed in Canada

ISBN: 978-1-4866-1664-0
eBook ISBN: 978-1-4866-1665-7

Word Alive Press
119 De Baets Street Winnipeg, MB R2J 3R9
www.wordalivepress.ca

MIX
Paper from
responsible sources
FSC® C103567

Cataloguing in Publication information can be obtained from Library and Archives Canada.

DEDICATION

After spending a considerable amount of time contemplating who to dedicate this book to, I concluded that it should be dedicated to my family, including my aunts, uncles, and cousins, as well as my parents, in-laws, sisters-in-law, brother-in-law, Carole, and Jeremy. Although not everyone is mentioned in the body of this book, I want to honor the people who are closest to me—my family and extended family.

Let me start with aunts and uncles. Two of the godliest women who I'm proud to call my aunts are Alberta (Birdie) Wood and Doris Haddock. Like my sister, they have been so supportive, and more importantly corrective, throughout my life. They are beautiful women who just love. Uncle Gert (Aunt Ena's husband) and Uncle Bruce (Aunt Doris's husband) have since passed away, but I fondly remember them and honor them. I haven't seen Uncle Jerry for many years, but I also include him in this dedication.

I also dedicate the book to Aunt Ena, Uncle Cor, Aunt Boujke, and Uncle Bill, who I rarely see but love and treasure. They have always been affirming and accepting of their nephew.

To my cousins and their children, Christine and her husband David, Heidi and her husband Shane, Frank, Ken, Peter and his wife Angie, Patty, Liz and her husband Rod, Gert, Joy, Paul, David, Ron, Ingrid and her husband Art. This is for you.

To Mark, Valerie and Vilma, and Carole's mom (Edith Wicks), my nephews Jordan and Jared, and my niece Melanie. This is for you, too. This is also dedicated to my father-in-law, Richard Wesley Wicks, who passed away in 2017. I miss you, Dad. You taught me, loved me, and showed me much. I want to thank you for Carole, the greatest gift you could have given me, on that Saturday, August 21, 1982. It would be a mistake to forget Carole's aunts, uncles, and cousins. They have treated me like their family. I've written this book for you also.

It has been such a tremendous blessing to have a family like this one. They are inclusive. They have been good to me and I honor each and every one of them with this book. Although you may not read their names, they have contributed to my life in ways I'm so grateful for.

Throughout this book, you will find photos to help you to relate to what I'm conveying. One of the traditions my wife Carole and I, as well as my parents, began was to have photos taken of us as often as we were together, since it wasn't frequent. Family was and is important to me.

PREFACE

When my father, Jacobus Telman, wrote the book *A Laugh and a Tear*, he had many years and experiences to draw from on two continents. He had a message to share that I believe is profound. The title came from his own father, Opa Telman, who used to say, "Life is a laugh and a tear," meaning that good and bad things happen to us all. The last sentence in that book was: "And so the story continues."

My father's book included sixty years of stories, including earth-shaking events. Some of those stories were so wild that I was inspired to ask him if they were true. He answered with a wink, saying that they really happened. With a shaky voice, Dad would also tell me of the horrors of war. He had been only nine years old when the Nazis invaded the Netherlands. Writing his book proved, not only to the reader but to himself, that life does have its tears, but it also has its joys.

As I close in on sixty years of life, I felt it was appropriate to write the sequel.

One of the ways my father expressed himself and experienced joy, in addition to writing, was to make music. He was a master musician who recorded four albums and played on numerous other albums. His love of music was overwhelming, so it's not a surprise that music also became a large part of my life.

Opa began my father on his journey of learning music at the age of four. Dad played piano like few could. He played tuba in the Salvation Army band and he could play accordion very well, but his real love was to play the organ. He so enjoyed it that most nights after supper he would announce that he was diving into Mozart, Bach, or Beethoven, which meant he was going to study and play the organ. Some years later, he found employment by playing for funerals and could tell stories of the weird and wacky services he attended.

If you peered into his shirt pocket, you would find a little notebook. In it were lists of appropriate songs for any event. His repertoire was massive, so hiring Jack Telman meant that you would have the most appropriate music at a highly satisfying quality. He played the accordion with such skill that he was invited to perform at dinner parties of government officials. He was invited to play for many events around Edmonton.

My father watching an Edmonton Oilers game.

My father even played for the Edmonton Oilers—not hockey, of course. I went with him to games and would prompt him when it was time to play the organ. I enjoyed meeting players like Wayne Gretzky and Mark Messier when they spent a game in the press box, which wasn't often.

He only played for two seasons. His complaint was not his pay but that he wasn't allowed to play "serious" music. When Dad handed in his resignation, the Oilers front office offered to raise his pay considerably, but Dad graciously declined.

A friend once suggested that he play Three Blind Mice when the players and referees took the ice. Most people could figure out that this wasn't advisable, but Dad was ignorant of what it could mean so he played it without me knowing. It didn't take long before NHL representatives were at the organ, giving him a tongue-lashing.

Dad was a classically trained church organist. He didn't know or even want to know other genres of music. He knew that Mozart and Bach wouldn't fit well for a hockey game, so he played what he knew. He played the gospel, including songs like "What a Mighty God We Serve", "This Is the Day," and "It Is Joy Unspeakable." Most fans wouldn't have recognized them, but they still enjoyed the joyous music. Christians, of course, would have loved it. It was like you were in church but with twenty thousand other people. To my knowledge, he was never told to stop playing these songs.

Dad was mischievous. One morning, he got up very early, went to one of the organs in the living room, and played the sound of a doorbell on it. Then he hid. When my mom got to the door, she found no one there. He did this a few times before she caught on.

Music was so much a part of our lives that one day, upon coming home from school, I found that there were no couches or chairs in the living room—just organs. Dad was in the habit of buying organs and pianos. When I questioned where I could sit, he simply said, "Pull up a bench."

Dad even built a dulcimer once. He brought us pan flutes, clarinets, saxophones, bugles, accordions, violins, and a myriad of other instruments for us to experiment with and ultimately have fun playing. Musical instruments were in abundance in our home, which made for a light-hearted atmosphere.

My father is most comfortable sitting at an organ. It's as if he can express his emotions clearly there.

Christmas was not a time to sing for our family. We simply played Christmas carols. Dad always grabbed the piano or organ bench first and the rest of us had to play trumpets, flutes, baritones, guitars, or other instruments that were lying around. Dad had us working, but we had as he challenged us with different songs and keys. His proficiency was so amazing. Most pianoplayers shake when asked to play in a key with sharps, but Dad found it easy. He was often asked to play in keys with up to six sharps. Not only did he do it with ease, he did it with a smile on his face.

Over time, Dad learned to play many styles of music, but his love was classical music. Along with Mom, he went monthly to see the symphony.[1] There he found healing for his heart. His desire was for me to also enjoy the beauty of the symphony, too, so he gave me his tickets occasionally. On my first date with my wife, Carole, we used Dad's tickets. Over the years, Carole and I have continued to attend the symphony in major cities throughout the world.

Dad also enjoyed marching bands. I believe this came from his years in the Salvation Army. I fondly remember him taking us to Empire Stadium in Vancouver to see a military band tattoo. On the football field, the band marched through their performance. Then, at the end of the concert, all of them marched out together and gave the audience chills at the magnificent music. I was quite young, but I'll never forget the thrill of watching a tattoo. Throughout my life, whenever I attend a parade, I watch for the bands and run to the front like a young child. I feel so much excitement when watching marching bands pass.

My father and I began playing duets when I was quite young.

[1] At one symphony concert my folks attended, the conductor lost his baton. It went flying into the crowd and landed on the lap of one of my parents' friends.

Quartets were also a passion for my dad. He took me to concerts of southern gospel, and even played piano for a gospel quartet. This gig lasted for more than twenty years. His playing was as impressive as the singing.

My awe of my father has never waned. He's always been my musical hero. Not only did he teach me music by example, he was also my first piano teacher. This carried on for a few years until he sent me on to other capable teachers.

While teaching, we began to play piano duets. Many years later, we continued to enjoy playing together. In his later years, he would take the bottom of the piano and I would take the top as we played four-handed song.

More than four decades later, my father and I still enjoy playing piano duets.

I wasn't the only recipient of his knowledge. My father owned a music school when I was young and he had dozens of students of the accordion, guitar, piano, and organ. Years later, it wasn't uncommon for someone to stop my dad in a store and tell him that many years earlier he had personally taught them. Dad was a very patient teacher. He had the ability to encourage and help students.

Dad was a master soloist, but he was also the perfect accompanist. He had the exceptional ability to make any performer sound great through his support. Mom played flute and Dad accompanied. I played horn and he accompanied. My sister Melody would sing, and Dad would accompany. He accompanied soloists in churches, concert halls, and hockey arenas. My people praised his ability to accompanying the vocals of our national anthem. He learned the anthems of many nations and beautifully played them before international hockey games.

My father was a master teacher of piano, accordion, and organ.

Additionally, he was a master composer. Several of his songs have been published, recorded, and sung by choirs around the world. The amazing fact is that he often wrote songs while watching television. *Hawaii 5-0* could be blaring, and Dad would sit there with his pencil and paper on the edge of the couch. One would think this would be impossible, but not for Dad.

In *A Laugh and a Tear*, Dad designated the chapters in a pattern I will loosely follow. The first chapter is also dedicated to the early years—in my case, the formative time in the 1960s and 70s.

My second chapter, like Dad's, will showcase the profiles of amazing people in my life, including my grandparents and my parents.

Chapter Three chronicles my school days, which span five decades. It's not that it took this long to finish grade school, though. Rather, the stories include events from my college, grad school, and post-graduate studies. It also includes my 17 years of piano lessons, nine years of trumpet/euphonium lessons, and ten years studying theology.

The fourth chapter is devoted to my wife Carole, and in it I share stories about our relationship. Carole has often been the inspiration for my writing. Our discussions, studies, and prayer times have reaped a bountiful harvest of wisdom. Chapter Five is devoted to my son, Jeremy. Carole and I weren't able to have children, and in 1989 we were blessed to adopt this beautiful person. Chapter Six is devoted to my sister Melody and her husband Brian.

In Chapter Seven, I describe the friends I have been blessed to know. My friends are of all ethnicities and live on all continents. Chapter Eight then includes a short record of my three decades of church ministry on three countries.

The epilogue concludes the book with my hopes and prayers for the reader. The intent of this book is not to praise any person but to inspire trust and belief in God, the creator who beautifully made us all with unique thoughts and ways. He is working in each one of us personally and lovingly.

My story is a testimony of God's faithfulness and kindness through every step of my life. I may not have struggled with drugs, alcohol, or other vices, but I have sinned—terribly sinned. I, too, have needed a savior. God didn't give up on me, but instead he has wonderfully and patiently worked in my life.

He is doing the same in your life, too. He is helping you even now. Throughout the book, you will read scripture and exposition that have helped me in my journey.

In my first book, *God's Riches and My Two Cents' Worth*, I shared the lessons I've learned through my years of church ministry. Some of the same stories and lessons from that book are sprinkled through this one.

If *Another Laugh and Another Tear* causes you to love God even more, it has been worth writing. I enjoy telling the story of God in my life. But my deepest desire is that this book will work like a springboard, lifting you closer to the creator. If along the way you giggle and shed a tear, I will take that as a bonus.

My parents always chronicled life by taking photos and keeping them in albums and on slides. Whenever I visited them, I would take a couple of these huge books and would sit down in the bathroom—yes, that's right, the bathroom, where I found solace and peace—and reminisce. Often a knock would come at the door and someone would ask if I could "hurry it up." When the door opened, whoever was standing there would cry out, "John has photo albums again!"

Later in the book, I'll talk about one album in particular that Mom and Dad titled "The Nut Gallery."

Words can help to describe events and people, but a picture goes a long way to draw the reader into the story. Of course, the faces of the people featured in this book have changed with age, but they represent how the person appeared at the time.

The life of John William Telman has been "a laugh and a tear," and there is no reason to believe that will ever change. I was known as a joker in my younger years, and I still have a healthy sense of humor and quick wit. But people also describe me, accurately, as a person who feels, loves, is thoughtful, and is inclusive. My desire has always been to make friends with anyone I encounter.

This has resulted in many laughs, but also many tears. I can fully attest to the fact that life has its ups and downs.

So, enjoy my story.

Chapter One
THE EARLY YEARS

Life in the Telman home could be accurately described as fun, safe, and precious. Mom and Dad laughed and loved, so arguments and tension were almost nonexistent. It wasn't a perfect home, but it sure was close. We prayed, we sang, we talked, and we played.

I was about three years old in this photo.

My first recollection is visiting my grandparents. We would pack the Volkswagen and head for Vancouver, where my mother's parents ran a home for men who were disabled in one way or another. Their home seemed huge to a small boy like me. It had many bedrooms, though, and the basement had a very large suite.

The backyard was like an endless forest for the mind. It had apple trees that produced bushels of sweet, juicy fruit. The apples that fell to the ground were heaven sent. Could it be that my love of apples stems from the aroma that captured me those many years ago?

In this huge yard, my grandfather built me a playhouse. It was more my size, compared to the enormous house. At the tender age of four, I imagined many things in that little house. It was *my* house, where I was king. And what did this king do? He looked at comic books, of course. The words were still out of reach, but the pictures were *neat*.

My grandfather was such a good sport. He marched in my band, as the only musician. We had so much fun. He would walk with me, hand in hand, down Hastings Street to buy a root beer float. He collected baseball cards for me, which I kept in an old bandage tin. Back in the day, bandages weren't sold in cardboard boxes. The tin was the perfect size for a little guy's collection. I also remember the popsicles my grandmother made with juice that she bought from the Fuller Brush Company. Life was so good.

My parents told me that when I was learning to speak, I frequently said, "I'm the boss." They had a tough-minded child to curtail, and in a hurry. It wasn't as bad as it may seem. They tell me that it made them laugh more than it concerned them. If I ever live like I'm the boss today, I'm sure Carole will quickly correct me.

Our home life was wonderful for my sister Melody and myself.

When I turned six, two monumental things took place. First, my sister Melody was born. She's my only sibling. As an adult, she has been the ideal sister. Melody has been my cheerleader, affirming me constantly. She truly has not seen my faults but has loved me unlike anyone else. At times her expressions of love have been embarrassing, but it comes from such a pure heart that it would be cruel to stop her from making them.

When we were children, we had fun, but we were natural enemies. No one could pinch like Melody, and boy could she scream when I defended myself. My ears are still ringing from her yells.

In her first few years, Melody had frightening troubles. She had seizures that at times left her temporarily blind and screaming in terror. How could I ever get angry at her when she suffered from epilepsy? My parents were equally fearful. So much was unknown, but to the glory of God Melody prayed and was eventually healed and didn't require medicine of any kind.

Along with the brain issues, she had trouble with her left side. To help her walk, she had surgeries to correct muscular abnormalities and wore a brace. In his book, Dad put it this way:

> We realized that something was wrong with Melody. She did not try to walk, and her left hand was immobile. We took her to the doctor who checked her out and said that there was nothing wrong with her. Nevertheless, we felt that something was wrong, so we took her to Edmonton's best pediatrician, Dr. Conradi. His assessment was that Melody had brain damage. It was a blow we never expected, and we were afraid for the worst. We were directed to Dr. Toupin, a neurologist, who determined that it happened at birth and affected the right side of the brain, which controlled the left side of the body. Her left hand and foot were uncontrollable. Melody did not walk until about two years of age, but she was a ball of energy. She could move around as fast on her bum with one foot behind and one ahead as any child on both feet. Her left hand never worked very well, but she became strong in the right hand and could pack a good punch.[2]

Dad also showed what our home was made of when our response to Melody's seizures got us to our knees: "We prayed in desperation. Soon we got used to those happenings and knew what to do."[3] During these troubles, we remained

---

[2] Jacobus Telman, *A Laugh and a Tear* (Edmonton, AL: Telman, 1989), 205.
[3] Ibid.

steady in our trust in the goodness of God and the healing that was going to come to Melody.

God did heal her. He did help her.[4] It has always been the belief of the Telman family to pray and place our trust in him.

Melody and I haven't only been brother and sister,
we've been best friends for our entire lives.

I must admit that all the attention Melody received could have made a brother bitter, but love wouldn't allow it. My sister is more than a sister. She's uniquely one who has shown me just how much God loves us and is working in our lives.

Melody could have become hard and selfish, but she didn't. She's become one of the sweetest people I've ever met. Her belief in the goodness and power of God is unprecedented. Few will trust God in the face of real trouble, but she has done so countless times. Her trust and love of God certainly hasn't reserved for her a smooth life, but that's the point. She is stubborn. She believes her God

---

[4] In Chapter Six, I'll share about how God healed Melody when she was near death decades later.

with no reservation. As much as she's been a cheerleader for my life, I honor her as a great woman of God.

My sister Melody and myself.

Before I turn to another topic, I'd like to mention an embarrassing moment that's come to mind. At one point, my parents shifted their affiliation from the Salvation Army to the Pentecostal Assemblies. We then attended a morning and evening service each Sunday. It was an exciting time that I'll look at in greater detail later, but for now I'll focus on one Sunday night when my mom and dad were running late and had packed us kids in the car quickly. On arrival at church, they noticed that Melody, who was an infant, didn't have a diaper on. Thankfully, there were diapers in the nursery. Melody has always been *cool*, but that night she was *cold*.

One special practice of our family, when I was young, was to watch the Jackie Gleason show on our twenty-inch black-and-white television each Saturday night. Melody and I spread blankets on the floor in front of the TV. Melody and I didn't understand the humor all that well, but Mom and Dad, sitting behind us on the couch, would have belly laughs.

In addition to Jackie Gleason, we watched Tommy Hunter, a Canadian country singer. In later years, I also watched hockey while the family did something else.

Saturday evenings were a time to prepare for Sunday. We would polish our shoes and Mom would put the breakfast dishes on the table. This created an expectation for the next morning.

So, the first monumental event in my life was the birth of my sister. The second one was my first year of grade school. Although I'll expand on this time in Chapter Three, I want to discuss a few aspects of it here. First, I was moving out into a world that wasn't safe and warm like our home, even if for just a few hours each week day. School was foreign and filled with challenges, including bullies. I had to confront my failure to live up to the expectations of the educational system. It didn't take long for me to be labelled as a slow learner, someone who was incapable of reading well. The principal of my school wanted me to have extra help and to be directed toward vocational programs. I wasn't expected to be able to keep up with the other students. This shook me.

Today, having graduated from high school, earned two bachelor's degrees, one master's degree, and a doctorate, it's gratifying to know that they were wrong.

Grade school was pivotal for me. On two occasions, I warranted punishment and was strapped by the school's vice principal. I was more than naughty, and I was often caught up in physical fights. One fight happened in class, and I can still remember the name of my combatant. He also was strapped. Most of the time when I fought, I ended up eating dirt and going home with torn cloths and a black eye. I had no fear that I would be in trouble when I got home, though. Mom would wash me up, hug me, and remind me that everything would be okay.

In the heat of the moment, things may seem bad, but God makes all things beautiful in their time (Ecclesiastes 3:11). I still see the faces of my opponents. In fact, one of my bullies eventually met Jesus Christ and went to Bible college. Another is a close friend now and a renowned lawyer.

One fight came about because I won a public speaking contest. I was eight years old and was awarded first place for my talk on being an immigrant's son. Two boys who didn't appreciate the result caught me after school and gave it to me with both barrels. Like other times, Mom cleaned me up and showed me the medal I won.

Another fight occurred right in the classroom. The teacher hadn't arrived yet when I started battling a boy whose name I still remember fifty years later. When the teacher came in, he took us both to the principal, who strapped us.

I didn't just anger other students. One teacher banished me to the gym showers for my quick tongue. When he later explained his reason for punishing me, I learned to be respectful of a teacher in front of other students.

Teachers could be severe with their punishments. Their frustrations towards students at times exploded. I still remember one teacher who grabbed students and shook them upside-down, or threw chalk or chalk brushes. We probably deserved it, but if teachers did that today they would be fired. I've never forgotten the name of the teacher who was so violent.

School wasn't the only place where I got into fights. I also ended up in tussles in the neighborhood. Once I must have been knocked out, since I woke with two children dragging me home.

Make no mistake, I wasn't always innocent. One time I tackled a girl who was running away and tore her shoulder. Another time I threw rocks over our yard's fence, and one rock found another child's forehead. That evening, Mom, me, and the next-door neighbor sat on his stoop to talk over what my punishment would be. There were times when Mom used a wooden spoon on my backside. Not once have I ever doubted her love, even when I felt her wrath.

Growing up in St. Albert, a suburb of Edmonton, was full of activities for us kids. We played road hockey in the winter and all the typical games, including hide-and-seek. I had a sneaky streak that profited me. I gathered all the kids together and found out they had all kinds of pets. They variously had turtles, hamsters, birds, dogs, and cats. I told them that we would build a zoo on my parents' front lawn. All the neighborhood animals were brought over, but who would pay to see the zoo? Why, the children with the animals. That's right. I charged the same kids a nickel to enter the zoo that had their own pet. What a slimy entrepreneur I was. Try not to laugh.

One Christmas, we all took sick. My creative father brought the mattresses from our beds into the living room, so we could spend Christmas together instead of being separated in our bedrooms. All day we lay on our mattresses and moaned with the television on. There wasn't a lot of interest in food or even presents that year. What strikes me is that our parents always wanted to create a home that was literally together in sickness and health.

At the tender age of six, I surrendered my life to Jesus Christ. I was in a Sunday School class when the invitation was given. I prayed with the teacher, and then in the Sunday morning service I again repented and dedicated my life to the Lord. The assistant pastor prayed with me.

That evening, we went to another church, and when the invitation was given I responded again. A kind lady there told me that I didn't need to make that decision again. I had been convinced that I was to take every opportunity to respond.

I floated in my relationship with God as I grew. At times, I was a passionate follower of Christ, and at other times I sinned miserably.

When my son Jeremy was just four years old, he asked, "Daddy, how can I go to heaven?" I explained it to him simply, and then I had the privilege to lead my son in the sinner's prayer. Carole was in the kitchen, weeping for joy.

As a youngster, I prayed and read my Bible every day, but sinned easily. God was so gracious to place godly people around me, including my family and schoolteachers, to help me in the journey.[5]

Only once in my formative years did my father ever strike me, and I know it truly hurt him more than it hurt me. He was crushed that he'd had to discipline me for my wayward mouth, and he later sent Melody to my room with a bag of Dutch licorice, my favorite treat. That was so like my dear dad. It was his way of saying, "Everything is fine, and forgotten." Every time I eat a piece of dark, double-salt Dutch licorice today I am reminded just how much my father loves me.

A significant reality of the Telman home was our lack of money. Dad worked three jobs and Mom worked up to two jobs just to keep our heads above water.[6] Financial pressures often fray relationships in a family, but not in ours. The fact that we didn't have much caused us to draw close to each other. When blessings came, like a bonus, we would dance around the living room as one.

Even though money wasn't in abundance, Mom and Dad found a way to pay for me to take piano lessons, trumpet lessons, and for Melody to take art lessons. The sacrifices our parents made was for more than just necessities; they sacrificed for us kids. Our parents were the best examples of selflessness.

Their kind-hearted love for others included a young boy named Pierre. As I mentioned, Mom and Dad never had a lot of discretionary funds available to them. But when they heard of another family's plight, they quickly responded with their limited resources.

Melody was often taken to the Glenrose hospital to deal with her disabilities. While there one day, they learned about a family who often had to bring their son Pierre to the hospital for treatment of his cerebral palsy. They lived on a farm some distance from Edmonton, which made it difficult to get to the hospital as often as they needed.

Mom and Dad became surrogate parents to Pierre. He lived with us for a time, and my parents made sure he made it to his appointments on time. This was no easy task, since Pierre needed significant attention on a continual basis—

---

[5] In Chapter Three, I'll mention one of my teachers who deeply impacted me for Christ during my teen years.

[6] Dad worked his day job, then taught music students (sometimes up to forty private students) and clean schools at night. Mom worked as a grocery store cashier during the day and at the post office at night. Various family members also delivered newspapers to supplement our household's meager income.

and he was heavy to pick up from the floor. Pierre couldn't walk, but he crawled and could get around quite easily. Along with Melody's difficulties and having a young son, my parents were pushed to great limits. They demonstrated godly character and evidenced love and kindness in their lives.

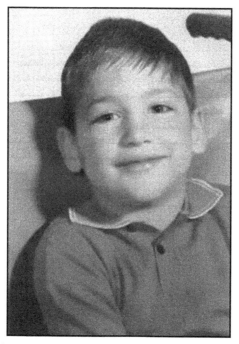

Pierre had disabilities but he also had a smile and a wonderful heart.

One day, Pierre went missing. We walked down the street only to find that Pierre had crawled to the neighbors' house just to get a hug. When asked why he had made his way to the neighbors, Pierre said, with an innocent look, "I just love people."

This was the world I grew up in. Out troubles and challenges were met with the fruit of the Spirit—love, joy, peace, patience, kindness, gentleness, goodness, faithfulness, and self-control (Galatians 5:22–23).

Financial pressures resulted in our family moving often. We moved at least seven times by the time I started high school. Dad said it this way in his book: "Life was a real struggle, but somehow we had a happy family and grew in the grace of the Lord."[7] He was right. Life was hard, but simultaneously it was joyous. We found ways to laugh and to be content with the little we had.

---

[7] Telman, *A Laugh and a Tear*, 215.

I don't know how our parents managed to do it, but when Melody and I begged for a pet, they found a way to get us a cat (that we all turned out to be allergic to), a hamster named Spotty (that didn't last long), and two dogs.

Pompeii was the first poodle Mom and Dad brought into our home, but he had a chronic toilet problem. Oh, the stories I could tell you but choose to avoid! You'd be glad that I won't tell you more about Pompeii.

Oh how we loved this beautiful dog. Mickey was family.

When I turned fourteen, we bought our second dog, Prince Mickey of Denmark, which was his official, documented name. Mickey was from a line of show dogs. He was a beautiful poodle and we had the joy of loving him for twelve years. Mickey, like the rest of the family, had several nicknames, including Mouse, Outhouse, and Louse. He was a well-trained dog who didn't mind being dressed up by us kids. Eventually he grew old, blind, had tumors, and developed a heart murmur. His pain grew to the point that Mom and Dad made the awful but necessary decision to relieve him of his pain. Dad wrote,

Since Mickey got sicker all the time and bumped into things, we felt it cruel to have him suffer more and made the difficult decision to have him put to sleep. I will never forget the day. It was like taking your child to an execution. We went to the vet, to at least talk about it, but while there we decided to go through with it right away. We kissed him one more time. He didn't know what was about to happen. On arriving home, we cried in each other's arms. He has never been out of our minds and hearts and represented some of our beautiful memories.[8]

Prior to entering Bible college, I had several jobs. Unlike some teenagers, I didn't have a paper route. I was too busy with music lessons, but during the summer months I held various jobs.

First I sold ice cream. This lasted one day, with my pay totaling one dollar. Even in the 70s, this was grossly little for a whole day's work. I also drove a rickshaw for a day. Again, the pay didn't match the energy expended, so I worked only one shift. A job that lasted longer was in the food services department of a hospital.

The most lucrative job was working as a bellboy at the McDonald Hotel in Edmonton, where I often made more than $100 in tips per shift. This made up for what I was paid, which was close to minimum wage. I could tell several stories of taking the luggage of celebrities to their rooms or welcoming royalty to the hotel. It was a fun job prior to beginning my time at Bible college.

Over the years, I also worked for the hotel giant Marriot. My job was to listen to agents on the phone and make sure that they maintained excellent customer service. I was pretty good at this job and earned two promotions in my first few months with the company.

In Canada, Tim Hortons rivals McDonalds for the number of stores in the country. In fact, even the United States now has several stores. While working there, I often took orders at the cash register. I couldn't help but minister to people, so I frequently observed people with pain written all over their faces. I would take prayer requests from them, and I also prayed for and counseled employees in the lunch room.

As an adult, I worked at the Edmonton International Airport as a "ramp rat." I was one of those guys who loads luggage onto the planes and waves planes in and out. My position was usually on the wing. One of my fellow wingmen wasn't observant one day, though, and a plane's wheel rolled over part of his steel-toed boot. Working as a ramp rat required one's full attention.

Most planes can reverse, but they don't often do it because the blast from the engines can damage terminal buildings. To avoid this, a small vehicle is

---

[8] Ibid., 280.

temporarily bolted to the plane to push the plane out. It turns the plane very slightly, so care must always be observed to make sure the vehicle doesn't flip and injure the driver. I never operated the push-back vehicle, and I'm glad. I drove other vehicles, though, including staircases.

One day I damaged a parked vehicle by not watching the angles when I made a turn. Nevertheless, it didn't take too long before I earned a promotion that required me to drive a truck up to a plane, open a hatch, connect a tube to the plane, and suck out the refuse from the lavatories. This was a less physical job and gave me a sense of independence that I enjoyed.

One winter, a large plane landed and I got to work. I drove my truck under the plane and moved the equipment up to the lavatory hatch. But the latch stuck, and when I tried to open the hatch, the refuse burst out all over me. It was in my hair, mouth, ears, eyes, in my pockets, and soaked right through my cloths. That was the worst experience of my life and immediately I was told to leave. When I got home, Carole told me to get in the shower with my boots and clothes on. Suffice it to say, I had a series of showers that day.

I learned a lesson from the incident: sometimes life poops on us, but we don't have to let it remain. We don't need to let the stink of others stick to us. Their smell is their smell. We can let God wash away the stuff of this life as we call on him to help us. His word washes us clean and he clothes us with clean clothes. He cleans us on the inside where we need it most.

My early years came to an end when I got married and moved out of my parents' home at twenty-three years of age. I couldn't have wished for a better upbringing. We didn't have money to go to Disneyland or to have the nicest cloths, but growing up in the Telman home was wonderful.

Venturing out on my own, I was full of grand expectations. Life had in many ways been a dream as I was growing up, but I would soon find out that my parents had sheltered Melody and me from many of the pressures and stresses they faced. It was time for me to grow up and become responsible for earning an income, paying bills, cleaning our apartment, and creating a home for my bride, future family, and myself.

The safety of my parents' home led my wife and I to return multiple times when we were in trouble, including periods being between jobs. Parents do this, don't they? They welcome their children back and help them. My parents were the best. Both Melody's family and mine received such care from them as adults.

My early years were wonderful. There were lots of laughs and tears, and especially a lot of love. Our family was strong not because of the absence of problems but because of the presence of God's grace through faith. It prepared Melody and me to face troubles of our own. It also helped us to build our own families based on certain principles that you'll notice throughout the rest of this book.

Now we'll place a microscope, so to speak, on the people who nurtured my growth: my parents and my grandparents.

Chapter Two

PROFILES

JACOBUS TELMAN (COOTJE, CO, DAD, FA-DUKE)

Our friends and family gather to celebrate my father's and my degrees.

Dad studied for many years to earn his degree in the organ at the Associate Royal Conservatory Toronto. Incidentally, he graduated at the same time that I earned my first bachelor's degree. It was a celebration time for our family.

My father, Jacobus Telman, was an immigrant to Canada from wartorn Holland. He was known as Jack, only to find out years later that his name should have been translated to James. He had no middle name. As a youth and a young man, his nickname was "Co." My opa, who was Jacobus Senior, was called "Black Co" because his skin was so dark.

To me, Dad was "Fa-duke." None of us knew where this nickname originated, since I was the only one to ever call him "Fa-duke." He was a personable man who spoke more with music than with his broken English. He almost had a funny look with thick glasses and little grin. Years later, Carole labeled it the "dumb dutchman" look.

He was born in Amsterdam in 1930 and witnessed the horrors of war in Europe. In his book, he described a lack of food, no heat, no light, and very little to do but try to endure. It has long been my belief that Dad often finished food left on other people's plates because he knew what it was like not to know where the next meal would come from.

My father is the eldest child on the left, with Uncle Cor and Aunt Ena when they were children in Amsterdam.

He tried to make the best of a frightening time, alongside his young sister Clasina (Ena) and younger brother Cornelius (Cor). In his book, Dad wrote about his view of World War II. He also shared how he and his siblings enjoyed life together. Frequently, siblings don't have good relationships, but they truly liked and loved each other. In their senior years, they were so excited to spend time together or to talk on the phone. You could always tell when my father was talking to his sister or brother because he began to speak loud, fast, and in Dutch.

The only time he spoke Dutch around our home was when he said a naughty word he didn't want us to know. If I had one complaint with him, it would be that he never taught us to converse in Dutch. He was so focused on integrating into Canadian culture and learning English that he wasn't inspired to teach us.

Although Dad was a proud Dutchman, he was equally, if not more so, proud to be a naturalized Canadian. After becoming a Canadian, he went to the Netherlands only once, with my mom. He had no interest in going back to his homeland. His disappointment with the many of troubles he'd heard about in the Netherlands changed his mind about the country for the worse. It would have been wonderful for him to lead us through the country and to show us the many sites, but he preferred to talk about the good days of the past and let go of the present.

The stories he shared with me showed just how fun life was in their home as he and his siblings were growing up. It would be a mistake not to tell two of the funnier experiences.

Dad told me that he and his brother and sister ran out of the house one fine day, playing tag and hiding from each other. He thought his brother ran back into the house, so he poked his head in the door and noticed the bathroom door closing. Unknown to him, that was a Salvation Army officer visiting his parents. Instead of running up to the door, he ran around to the side of the house to the bathroom window, found a stick, slightly opened the window, and jammed the stick through. Imagine the horror when he found out that the officer was sitting in the bathroom and not his brother!

Another funny story involving these three mischievous kids took place at the home of a relative. Dad and his siblings were put to bed upstairs one evening while the adults visited downstairs. Like most children at bedtime, they tried to delay sleep by calling for a cup of water. The lady of the house scolded them and announced that the next sound from them would mean a spanking.

A little while later, my uncle whispered, "I have to go to the bathroom." The bathroom was downstairs, and he would have to get past the adults to get to it, so he asked my dad what he should do. Dad was the eldest, so surely he would know. The story goes that my father told him he couldn't leave the room, so he should do his business and throw it out the window. Apparently he did, but then his problem was that his hands were soiled. Dad said, "Now you have to go downstairs."

Attempting to be as quiet as possible, my uncle tiptoed down the stairs with his hands on the railing. The lady saw him and went running up the stairs after him only to get her hands dirty. Suffice it to say, it didn't go well for Uncle Cor or my father.

I have a difficult time believing these stories, but he claims they happened. Who knows? I've never ventured to ask my aunt or uncle, for fear of hearing more fanciful stories. The Telman family knows how to tell stories—and they may not always be true to life.

Dad never lost his Dutch accent, so I often had fun when he mispronounced words such as *developing* (devil upping) or *maracas* (mark ahs). I could never figure out if he was being genuine or if he was playing with me, since he always had that innocent, boyish grin. Carole says that I have developed a similar look.

When Carole and I were married, Dad, the man who said, "If you ain't Dutch, you ain't much," gave us wooden shoes. They have decorated the front entrance to every home we've ever had.

Dad had distinct and somewhat strange tastes. He didn't like drinking water, so he would have coffee, tea or diet ginger ale. Like his own dad, he didn't like tomatoes. Both would gag when someone even mentioned them. This was strange, since he liked tomato sauce on pizza. He hated spaghetti, though. Mom had to be highly creative with her meal plans because of what Dad would and wouldn't eat. I thought some of the things he enjoyed were unpleasant, such as a vegetable called "broad beans."

I'm proud to be the son of Jacobus Telman (no middle name).

He had no known enemies, since he looked to make people his friends. He did this in unassuming ways, including through music but also through his innocent ignorance. He was also funny, having a great sense of humor that endeared him to people. He once told me, "If you get someone to laugh at you, they will be less likely to punch you in the nose." I often heeded this little bit of wisdom, and it did help at times. It's difficult to be angry at a person who doesn't post a threat, for his stature was well under six feet. He did develop a large belly, but most people towered over him. He didn't look like trouble, but neither did his looks attract people.

Despite his look and speech difficulties, Dad became quite popular. I mostly attribute this to his amazing musical talent. In addition to playing piano and organ, he played tuba, which went back to his time in the Salvation Army in his native Holland. In Canada, he again joined the Salvation Army and played tuba, but later he became the bandmaster in Edmonton. Incidentally, his bandmates included Carole's uncle and grandfather.

Wedding photo of Dorathy Huckle and Jacobus Telman.

It was in the Salvation Army that Jack Telman met Dorathy Huckle. Both were officers in the Army. Jack was smitten. He had moved to Canada hoping to find and marry a North American Indian girl. In the books he'd read about Canada, these women had looked so beautiful to him. But when he saw Dorathy, who wasn't Native, he stopped looking. With her raven hair, he realized that he had found the beautiful wife he had crossed the Atlantic to find. Although it was love, Mom did admit to having a fair bit of pity for this funny little man.

Music has always been a great part of my dad's life. Sports, on the other hand, wasn't important to him until I showed an interest in hockey and football. Dad made a huge effort to enter my world. Many times, he and I went to football games together. We would sit at Clark Stadium and Commonwealth Stadium, in all kinds of weather, to watch the Edmonton Eskimos. He learned the game and soon became engrossed in the team. After I moved away, every year he sent me a team sticker and schedule for the upcoming season. What a dad! His willingness to join me in something I enjoyed spoke volumes of his unquestionable love for me. It was just another point of contact that solidified our relationship. I hold him up as one of the best examples of what a father should be.

My father has always had a great sense of humor.

When I was three years old, a picture of me and my dad made it into the *Edmonton Journal* newspaper. In the photo, I'm sitting inside the tuba while Dad blows as hard as he could. I wish I could remember what that was like! My father was so much fun.

I sure wish I could remember when my dad and I played horsie on the beach.

One football game he and I went to stands out in my memory, and the memory has nothing to do with the Edmonton Eskimos on the field. We parked a few blocks from the stadium and walked to the gate. We saw no reason that we couldn't park there, but when we returned the car was gone and we saw a No Parking sign hanging from a nearby tree. Dad was furious. I laughed as we walked downtown to the police station, where he announced to an officer that someone had stolen our car. After checking, we were informed that it was the police who had "stolen" it, by towing it away. After that, we were more careful about where we parked.

I may have inherited my father's mischievous ways. One day at his home, a group of us was visiting in the living room. That's when I took the opportunity to have some fun and tied everyone's shoes together. When Dad got up to go for his typical walk, he sat right down on the floor to untie his shoes. He didn't become angry at the inconvenience. He simply went along with the fun.

Dad was never much of an athlete. He tried throwing a baseball and football, and his heart was always toward his children, but he lacked the skills to participate in sports. He would rather watch. I once asked him to kick a soccer ball around with me. Even though he wasn't an athlete, being a father motivated him to try. Almost immediately he missed the ball and injured himself by severely pulling his groin. He was wearing shorts and the bruise began to show instantly. It went all the way down his leg. It hurt me to see him in such pain, but my father never resisted playing with his son.

Dad told me that my first solo at church was "Jesus Loves Me."

Dad never did drugs or drank alcohol, so he was in good health until he began suffering from type-2 diabetes in his later years. He managed it quite well by walking a fair amount every day and controlling his diet. In his 70s, he battled cancer, had a minor stroke, and years later had hip replacement surgery. Dad always seemed to smile through the discomfort.

On a typical winter day with snow falling gently to the ground, Dad went for his usual walk but slipped on the ice and broke his ankle. The pain was so acute that he passed out in a snowbank. Some kind young people saw him and took him to the hospital, where he received surgery to repair the damage. For an elderly man who exercised by walking, this was devastating.

Dad always enjoyed walking because of the beauty of God's creation, so being cooped up was a frustration to him. After the ankle mended, he returned to his daily practice of walking. In the winter, he avoided potential problems by walking in his and Mom's building at Summit Village.

What many may not know is that my Father was also an artist who dabbled in pencil drawing and painting. Since music was his love, he drew great composers. They are almost like caricatures that exaggerate their features.

Bach, Beethoven, Liszt, and Brahms were a few of the drawings that hung in his TV room.

Dad also liked to paint scenery. Some he painted from pictures he saw, and others were painted onsite. They were given to us kids as gifts with frames. We treasure them even now. In Brian and Melody's home, they hang the paintings down a hallway and call it the Jack Telman gallery.

Throughout my life, I've known my Father to speak little bits of wisdom. For example, "If you see someone drowning, you do not let him pull you in. You reach in and pull him out," "You cannot condone what God condemns," and "If it doesn't go one way, it's bound to go the other."

For his eighty-fifth birthday, we invited many friends to come celebrate. We had a cakemaker design a birthday cake that looked like an organ. Even the pedals, bench, and sheet music were edible. It was amazing. Not only did it taste wonderful, but it was enough to feed fifty people.

Dad was creative in various ways, including integrating music and games. He created his own board game, Music Masters of the World, which was like Trivial Pursuit except the game pieces moved along a musical staff.

*My dad and his friend Jim entertained people at
the world-famous West Edmonton Mall.*

Dad and a friend of his, Jim, once saw an advertisement for a talent competition in which seniors were asked to enter. It was almost unfair, since they were both exceptional musicians, but they participated and won, not surprisingly. I don't recall the prize, but to them that wasn't the point. Dad and Jim just enjoyed making music. Incidentally, Jim was also a Dutchman.

Lovable Jack Telman.

My father, Jacobus Telman, was a man with faults but with the fingerprint of God on his precious life. As I watched him age, my heart couldn't have been drawn more to this wonderful man. When I had occasion to visit my folks, I loved going for walks and spending time with my dad at a local coffee shop. Cell phones and computers have meant very little when I had the privilege of hearing him tell me stories of the old country and his many experiences. Others may struggle with family relationships, but for me I deeply loved my father.

DORATHY ELIZABETH TELMAN (MOM, MRS. DRIPPY NOSE, DOT, BETTY)

My dear mother, Dorathy Telman. Notice that her name is spelled unusually.

To describe this woman accurately would require the most superlative words imaginable. Dorathy Huckle was born in Calgary—and note the spelling of her name, which is different from the common spelling. She and her siblings—two sisters, Alberta and Doris, and brother Bill—lived with their parents on a farm in central Alberta. They were churchgoing people and hard workers. Some might call them typical country bumpkins, but this shouldn't be taken negatively. Instead the Huckles could be understood as unpretentious. In some ways, they were much like the Telman family, all the way over in Amsterdam.

Mom has had her share of difficulties, but the result has been pure gold. Just as fire refines, she has come through her troubles with grace, beauty, and elegance. Some people would have been destroyed by the fury of troubles she endured. Dorathy Elizabeth Huckle not only endured, but she became better because of her indominable spirit of faith and love.

Like Dad, she was always fun-loving and kind. On a snowy winter day, Mom once took her little ones sledding down a hill only to knock out a tooth. She used to joke with us—and most of all, laugh with us. Her infectious personality drew us to her. Having friends was great, but spending time with Mom was truly a highlight of my life. It didn't hurt that she was an exceptional cook. Her desserts were tastier than anything you could purchase at a five-star restaurant.

Mom was always a good sport and helped anywhere she could. If Dad needed another musician, she would step in with a smile and a gentle heart.

Mom, second from the right in second row, playing in the band at church.
I'm standing to her right, and Dad is conducting.

One might expect that most of my musical education came from my father, but Mom was no slouch when it came to musical knowledge and proficiency. She played the tuba, the baritone, and in her later years she took flute lessons. She could read music, play the piano, and was a competent teacher.

One day I came home with a problem. The youth pastor at our church, Greg Wyton, who still is a friend after all these years, heard that I had taken some years of piano lessons and he asked me to play for the youth service. Until then, I had only learned to play classical music. I moaned about my lack of ability to my mom, but she had a plan. She told me to sit at the piano with a hymnbook.

"Open the hymnbook and play something," she said. "Then shut it and play it again."

"But Mom, I would need to memorize it," I complained.

Her response has stuck in my mind for decades. "You can play it even if you haven't memorized it, since it's in your heart and mind."

From that moment on, I was able to play by ear. The first song I played by ear was a hymn, and the second was "I Believe In Music" by Mac Davis.

Incidentally, I did play for the youth service that week. It wasn't smooth and strong, but I had turned a corner which led to easily playing all styles of music by ear or by music.

All of us had nicknames. Mine was Stoop.[9] Melody had numerous nicknames, including, Bum, Skootch, Bose, and other unexplainable monikers. Even Carole had a nickname, Swittie, which was the result of me fumbling over words.

I should explain my mom's nickname, Mrs. Drippy Nose, which came from her allergy problems. She would often smile with a Kleenex in hand. She eventually had surgery to correct a nasal problem and her drippy nose disappeared.

Incidentally, I had the same surgery on my nose many years later.

Mom was a master cook. Her desserts were amazing. It was always a treat to go home to dig into what she served. Why go out to eat when you could sit at her table? All the love she put into her creations made mealtime a thrill. Not only was the food nutritious and tasty, it was presented with elegance and charm. The table always had her attention. She was the last to eat and she ate slowly. We had to stay at the table until everyone was finished, so this was Mom's sneaky way of gently extended our family time.

Dad, on the other hand, wasn't a cook in any world. When Mom was away, Dad would attempt to cook—and we still laugh at his dessert creations. One

---

[9] I asked if this was short for Stupid and was reassured, with a wink, that it wasn't.

culinary experience still stands out in my mind. Dad cooked the largest tapioca balls with rhubarb. It was horrible. He tried to cook eggs and failed there, too. Dad always depended on Mom's excellent cooking.

One tradition in the Telman family was to have pancakes on Saturday mornings. Mom filled them with raisins. After saying or singing the blessing, often in Dutch, the tradition included taking a pancake in hand and singing the following little song together: "Pancakes, everyone. Pancakes, everyone. We know how to eat them." Then we would slap the pancake on the plate. I'm not sure anyone knows how this crazy but fun tradition became a part of our family, but everyone enjoyed it and participated with a giggle.

We often sang a prayer of grace before eating, in Dutch: "Fader, wij danken U. Fader, wij danken U. Hemelse Vader, wij danken U." Translated, this means, "Father, we thank you. Father, we thank you. Heavenly Father, we thank you." I've since learned that the song has three verses. We only sang the first, but the song is a beautiful expression of thanks. Remembering that Dad and his family sang this even when food was scarce has taught me that food, that all we have, should be taken with a grateful heart.

I don't know the names of some dishes we ate, but they were tasty, filling, and elegantly presented. Mom even learned to cook Dutch food that any Dutchman would love.

There was only a few desserts of hers that I tried to avoid, an almond-based Dutch pudding. She also served marzipan cookies that I couldn't stomach. Other Dutch treats I always looked forward to, like double salt licorice, croquets, and oliebollen. This proves to me that although I have Dutch blood, I'm a Canadian with discerning taste.

On New Year's Day, in a year I don't recall, she went skating and severely broke her wrist in a fall. This as well as all other accidents and troubles didn't negatively impact her character. In bad and good, she has always remained a jewel of great worth. She was unshaken because her kids were all right. Even when trouble hit others, she was there at the front of the line to help.

One night, we were awakened by horrible screams. No, it wasn't another seizure that hit Melody. Across the alley from our house, a tent was on fire. Some children, like many of us were apt to do, had pitched a tent in their backyard. As the story goes, some young people had walked by in the night and thrown a firecracker on the tent to surprise the kids. Sadly, the tent had exploded into an inferno that consumed the children in the tent. Mom went running out while Dad, Melody, and I stood at a bedroom window. Mom didn't go into detail in our presence, but I did overhear her tell Dad that the faces of those dear children were melted off.[10]

September 30, 1977 was another fateful evening. That night, we received a horrible call telling us that my cousin Dale, a young boy of twelve, had died in a tragic accident. Mom immediately sprang to action and headed off to the United States to be with her sister Alberta and her husband Jerry. Mom had this way of being a comforting blanket for those who were in real pain. She never had overly profound things to say, although she had great bits of wisdom. But she had the amazing ability to empathize and attach herself to others so that they had someone to help carry their burden.

My mother was an officer in the Salvation Army.
Her ministry was serving in a children's home in the mid-1950s.

Although Mom didn't write a book or play music for mayors, she still had her place and contribution. Mom wrote the following poem, which paints a picture of the serenity and peace found in her home.

---

[10] The story of this tragedy is told by one of the victims, Dave Hammer, in his memoir, *From Out of the Flames* (Winnipeg, MB: Word Alive Press, 2011).

CONTENTMENT WITH OUR PLACE

It's an evening in summer and the balcony's our place
Temperature is balmy, sky is blue, a few fluffy white clouds
Just a breeze to make the trees come alive
Hard to believe that in a mad world there's such a place of peace
A squirrel runs over the power line and then to a tree
People walk by with a tiny dog on a leash
Close by are a few teens sitting, talking and laughing together
People walk by say a cherry, "hello"
Our birdie flies by to check on his birdhouse
While a plane flies high in the sky
A beautiful blue jay announces his arrival
The fragrance and colorful beauty of the flowers
To complete this peaceful scene
Beautiful flute and harp music in the background
What more do we need?
We are blessed.

Mom is such a sweetheart.

This strong woman wasn't deterred by her age. As mentioned, she took up the flute in her late seventies. With the help of Dad writing music for her, she played beautifully. The flute isn't an easy instrument to play, especially for a senior.

In the 1990s, Mom had a brain tumor and needed surgery. The night before, I was a wreck, which shocked me. My trust is in God, but this was my mother and she faced the possibility of losing her eyesight, hearing, and a change of personality. Worse, she could have died. That night, I called my friend, Sam Ramphal, and asked him to pray with me.

The next day, she made it through the surgery with only two issues. For the rest of her lovely life, she complained of a dent in her head. "Feel this hole in my head," she would say, directing my hand to it. I just cringed to feel the dent. She also said that her head often felt "tight." We guessed that her skin was stretched in an uncomfortable way.

Like Dad, Mom never did drugs or drank alcohol, so her health was good. She did have a minor heart attack and skin cancer in her later years, but she dealt with these health issues by eating well and walking.

My love for her increased by watching her heart of pure love for others. I could mention so many examples of this, but suffice it to say that she is one of the best God ever created. You could sense the shine of God's glory emanating from her. She is an excellent example of what God is like. The story of her life threads its way through this book not only because she is a hero of mine but also because her character is hard to hide in the life of our family.

Me and my mom.

As a young boy, I knew she loved me. I wanted her to know that I loved her also, so one Saturday evening I asked if she would go for a bike ride with me. She said yes. I didn't tell her where we were going, but I led her to an ice cream parlor and bought her an ice cream. We sat and talked as friends would.

As an adult, Mom has been a trusted friend I could talk to and find a listening ear. More than once, when I was in financial trouble, she and Dad would come to my rescue without flinching. I learned that it would have been fruitless to argue.

She was always on the front row when I was performing in school plays or piano recitals. She covered many miles on a bus with me to get to music lessons, and even to play hockey one year. Her support and belief in her only son was unmistakeable. There's nothing like the love of a mother.

JACOBUS TELMAN (PATERNAL GRANDFATHER, BIG CO, BLACK CO, OPA)

This is my grandfather, Jacobus Telman, at my wedding in 1982.

I knew Opa as a kindly man who knew his God. He had a gentle expression and had the same "dumb Dutchman" look he must have passed on to my father. He was so dark that he looked like he was from the Middle East. This was troubling during World War II. Would the Nazis assume that he was a Jew? His nickname was Black Co, because of his skin tone.

Back in the Netherlands, he had been a master builder, and the Nazis had forced him into labor. When he didn't get home at a reasonable time, the family would be deathly worried that he'd been sent to a concentration camp. Thankfully he made it through the war and eventually settled in Vancouver, Canada.

Even though I sat and talked with him many times, the thing I remember most about him is his back. Opa had the habit, a habit which my dad also developed, of often going for walks by himself. He would start his day with a long walk, then go for additional walks throughout the day. So when I had the opportunity of visiting him, I usually saw his back walking away. He treasured these quiet times of solitude. No doubt it was his time of prayer and listening to God.

Speaking of his father, my dad wrote,

Father was well respected in the Pentecostal church where he became the choir secretary and a board member. He was always very quiet and never got excited but always had something good to say so they listened to him. Father read his Bible faithfully every day which soon was marked up from cover to cover. I remember him sitting at the table every morning before going to work and reading the Bible. His interest was especially in Israel and the prophets...

He worked very hard and often times came home exhausted and wet from the rain. In that time, construction had to be done mostly by hand. It was not a picnic. Yet he always had time to tuck us in at night after romping around with us and chasing us all over the place.[11]

Prior to my birth, my father's mother died, which was very difficult for Opa. But God had someone else to help him through his later years of life. We'll talk about Femme later in this chapter. She was the only paternal grandmother I knew. Dear Opa was strong but had a difficult time adjusting to his wife dying and marrying again at a later age, but he did his best.

Some years after Opa and Oma immigrated to Canada, Opa took sick. He eventually became a victim of Alzheimer's disease, which was most difficult for the family. He knew scripture and he knew hymns, but at the end he didn't know his family.

Opa, like my father, was a musician who played the organ and the flugal horn. He was a member of the Salvation Army and played in the band. I fondly

---

[11] Telman, *A Laugh and a Tear*, 15.

remember him sitting at his little organ, playing hymns. Dad wrote, "Father brought most of the music into the family."[12]

My years with Opa were few. We didn't see each other that much, but when we did it was wonderful. While the other grandchildren were playing, I loved sitting at his feet and listening to him quote scripture and sing hymns.

Opa loved to walk. Early in the morning, he would get his walking stick and head off. At times he would walk an hour one way. Both Opa and Dad eagerly encouraged others to join them on their walks. This wasn't only exercise; it was also a way to enjoy the beauty of Canada. There was so much to see and people to talk to.

My father wrote,

In 1988, Opa Telman was not doing too well and my relatives thought that he may not last too long. So, we decided to make a trip to Vancouver in March. We were so glad that he recognized us. We realized how hard it was for him, knowing how dependent he was on everybody. For Cor and Boukje, it was time-consuming and hard work, and of course Ena was involved also and tried to visit him as much as possible. For Oma, it was not easy, but at least she rented a suite across from the hospital, so that she could look after him each day. Father was often frustrated and longed for the end and the beginning of glory. At last, the Lord took him away in July 1988. We flew down and attended the funeral. Oma was very strong, but our hearts were hurting for her. I played the organ and people sang Father's favorite song, "How Great Thou Art."[13]

I was told that Opa was anxious to leave this world. During his final days, he often said, "I just want to go to be with my God." He could see that there was something ahead. He may have been impatient for his death, but he was not discouraged. He was still singing hymns and quoting scripture.

One of the most moving memories of my life comes from attending his funeral in Vancouver. Many of our relatives were there, but I stayed close to Mom and Dad. At the funeral, my father played the organ with such loving tenderness, beauty, and excellence. Remember, it was Opa who had begun my father on his musical journey.

---

[12] Ibid., 16.
[13] Ibid., 311.

My grandfather's graveside.

The funeral had to be difficult for Dad, because he loved his father as much as I love mine. Being the eldest, he had been very close to his father. It deeply touched my heart to watch my father grieve. Standing at my grandfather's graveside has given me a picture of what it will be like to say goodbye to my own dad someday.

NEELTJE TELMAN (NE. BEENAKKER, PATERNAL GRANDMOTHER, OMA)

My grandmother passed before I was born, so her photo means much to me.

I never knew my Oma, as she passed away before I was born. So I will depend on the words of my father:

Mother was the youngest of three sisters and two brothers. She lived most of her life close to her parents. Mother seems to have had the dreamlike nature of her father, which in turn she passed on to me. I have her brown hair and blue eyes, and to a certain extent her complexion. Mother had a beautiful alto voice and she used to play the alto in her younger days. She had a big heart for the whole world and she proved that many times over.

Towards the end of the war we used to say that after the war we would immigrate to California where the oranges grow on the trees. We ended up in Canada where the frost grows on the trees, but Mother was never meant to see the "new world."[14]

It was touching to read what my father wrote about his mother, but I will limit his quotes to how he remembers the final few months of her life:

My mother started to put on weight again after the lean war years, but with that also returned an old problem, gallstones, that caused her lots of suffering. Soon she was getting attacks on a daily basis and vomited each time. Her pain was so horrible that even the neighbors could hear her screams. In March of 1949, it was evident that mother did not have long to live. One evening we went with the Corps cadets to the hospital to sing for mother. We sang in the hallway just outside her room. I remember that we sang "Abide with Me" and several girls started crying. I remember how Mother's lips were always dry and we were only allowed to moisten them.

I believe it was on a Saturday and we were all together at home with our relatives. Father was in the hospital to spend the end with Mother. We said goodbye the day before, but it was hard for her because she didn't want to let go of us. To make it less traumatic, Father was alone with her on that Saturday. It gave them some final moments together, which was good. Sometime later, he arrived looking like a different and older man. All he said was, "It's over."[15]

---

[14] Ibid., 16–17.
[15] Ibid., 85.

My father has always spoken glowingly about his mother. His love for her is like that of a father's love for his eldest child. He had a deep, close relationship with her which is similar to the one I believe I've had with my own mother.

Oma was so young when she passed, which is sad for all of us. We lost the joy of knowing this beautiful woman who Dad had a brief few years with. I look forward to meeting her in the life to come. I have been told that I resemble her.

Some believe I look much like my father's mother. What do you think?

FEMMIGIE TELMAN (NE. PAASM, PATERNAL STEP-GRANDMOTHER, OMA)

Like Carole's father's father, my dad's father remarried after the death of his wife. This strong woman became my grandmother.

Dad wrote of his stepmother, "I was relieved for Father that he had someone to look after him again."[16] She was younger and capable of helping Opa and his three children. Interestingly, Carole's paternal grandmother also passed away and her grandfather also remarried later in life.

Oma was a fireball of honesty and frank speaking. She often walked down the street behind an overweight person and say out loud, "Het hele huis is van mij van deze kant naar deze kant," which roughly means, "All the house is mine from this side to this." Imagine having a little old lady walk up behind you speaking in a foreign language. This was a way in which she would mock someone in a funny way.

While she was bold and strong, she also had a kindly demeanor. She loved and cared about people, especially her family. My father called her Mother because she wasn't a substitute. She was Oma.

Taken when Opa and step-Oma came to visit us. I was fifteen years old.

After Opa passed away, she moved back to the Netherlands and lived out her years on the coast where she enjoyed the sea. Like my other grandparents, she lived a long life. She reached her one hundredth year but was suffering with blindness and a weary body. Most of her family were in Canada or dead, so she was ready for promotion.

---

[16] Ibid., 118.

JOHN HAROLD HUCKLE (FRATERNAL GRANDFATHER)

My grandfather was such a godly man.

I would fail to find any human being as godly as John Harold Huckle, my mom's father. It was my honor to preach at his funeral. There was so much to say about his ways, ways which we should all emulate.

He was a joker who was quick to dance a jig. He often had a fun story to share. He always smiled and showed unparalleled love for everyone, including his wife who publicly treated him horribly. She didn't only correct him, she threw verbal daggers. Instead of striking back or sulking, he returned good for abject evil.

I attribute this to his incredible character because of his love and relationship with God. On many occasions, I saw him weep uncontrollably when he heard the name Jesus. I'm convinced that when he returned good for evil, he was worshipping God. Paul the apostle wrote, *"Never pay back evil for evil to anyone. Respect what is right in the sight of all men… Do not be overcome by evil, but overcome evil with good"* (Romans 12:17, 21) Grandpa Huckle must have taken this to heart. He lived it and was a wonderful example of what a Christian should be.

My Grandpa loved to play the fiddle.

I fondly remember his singing. He had a gentle, fatherly voice that was so enjoyable to listen to, especially when he sang songs such as "When Jesus Comes," "I'd Rather Have Jesus," and "No One Cared for Me Like Jesus." The second verse of this last song is most significant when you know a little bit about my grandfather:

> No one ever cared for me like Jesus
> There's no other friend so kind as He
> No one else could take the sin and darkness from me,
> O how much He cared for me.[17]

My wife and I have a long-play album of him singing some of his favorite hymns. He sang in church, and every time he came to the word Jesus, you guessed it, he would weep. Powerful was the moment. Even now I get chills thinking about the impact of the instant Grandpa sang "Jesus." He loved the Lord like no one I've ever met.

Grandpa was a believer in the King James Version of the Bible. He didn't mind the old English and felt that the new versions watered down the impact of its message. Who was I to argue with such a godly man who treasured the Bible more than he treasured his bankbook?

Whenever possible, Grandpa liked to play games with me, including ping pong and sjoelbak, a Dutch shuffleboard game. His favorite game was chrokinole,

[17] Dr. Charles Weigle, "No One Cared for My Like Jesus," 1932.

a game where little wooden discs are flicked into a center hole. Grandpa was at his best when he was playing this game with his grandchildren.

He worked on the railway of Canada, where he damaged a finger on his left hand while working in a brass foundry. This was the hand he used to play the fiddle. After that, the finger was always curled from the nerve damage. It didn't deter him. And he continued to enjoy playing the violin.

Grandpa had such a great sense of humor.
This allowed him to dress up and play with us kids.

As I stated earlier, Grandpa Huckle was always a good sport. He got involved in my life with the things I wanted to do, which endeared him to my heart.

Whenever someone scooped some butter off a dish, he would scrape the butter off their knife and take it for himself. We all giggled when he did this. It emphasizes the theme of this book, that life is a laugh as much as it's a tear. The butter-scraping incidents may not seem like much on paper, but to those of us who saw him do it, it proved that he had a fun, loving, mischievous streak.

He also loved ice cream and fudge, probably more than most. He could make his own tasty homemade fudge. He taught me to ride my bicycle and he liked to dance; it was a happy dance, what we called a jig.

My father playing the according, with Grandpa playing the violin.
Grandma is visible in the mirror.

Despite how he was treated by his wife, he lived a life of joy and peace. What a remarkable man, and what an example to his children and grandchildren and to everyone who knew him. I'm proud to be counted as one of his grandsons.

CAROLINE HUCKLE (FRATERNAL GRANDMOTHER)

Grandma was a study in extremes. She could give with such liberality yet exaggerate and be unkind to her husband. It would have shocked anyone.

Grandma Huckle

To Grandma, though, I could do no wrong. Even if I kicked a dog, she would say, "He had it coming." I could have milked her attention and kindness towards me, but when I witnessed the way she treated my grandfather, I did everything I could to talk to her about my faults.

Occasionally I would visit for lunch. My office wasn't far, so I enjoyed taking breaks to spend time with Grandpa, who was a beautiful person, and Grandma, who adored me. When I arrived, Grandma wouldn't have prepared sandwiches or soup; she would have cooked a turkey with all the fixings and apple pie. It truly was a feast, and it happened every time I came for lunch. I felt like royalty.

"Grandma," I would say, "please don't make a fuss for me."

She would look at me like she didn't understand. To her, it only made sense to put on a spread for her "Johnny boy." My grandfather didn't complain, since he too would receive an amazing lunch.

Grandma often talked about who she knew as if she had relationships with the most important people in the world. This wasn't just old age speaking; we all knew she had problems with reality.

Sadly, her death also came with great sadness. Here's where I shed a tear.

In her last months, she denied that she had any family at all. Her children loved her despite her denial and always wanted to show her that they cared—but she resisted close relationships. One wonders what caused her to feel this way. Had she had a tragic childhood? She'd stated that she had been sexually abused by her father and even saw him die. In later years, the family found out that personality disorders are often a result of sexual abuse. Could this explain her mental troubles?

No one really knew her real age. She claimed that she was older than the family speculated. Grandpa dared not discuss Grandma for fear of her sharp tongue.

In her work at the nursing home, she showed the ability to be kind and loving, if she wanted to. As a small child, I once witnessed her taking charge and helping a man who was having a severe seizure. The internal struggle the family had with her was always difficult and could cause tears, though. She could be extremely kind or extremely mean. There was no middle ground for Grandma.

Before her death, she gave up eating. It wasn't anorexia that took hold of her. She just decided that she didn't want anything at all. She didn't want love, and she didn't want the things that were necessary to life itself. She was mentally ill and we all knew it. Nevertheless, we loved her.

It was painful for my mother both while Grandma lived and when she passed.

For all of Grandma's faults and illness (she also had chronic bowel trouble), she can be commended for raising her children. She wasn't perfect by any stretch, but my aunts and mother, became wonderful women of God, and my Uncle Bill is a kind man who served others as a paramedic. Grandma did something right.

Chapter Three
SCHOOL DAYS

I mentioned earlier that educators weren't optimistic about my future as a student. Remember, I often got into fights. Added to this was my apparent difficulty reading. The prospect of me going on to continued education was low, according to some, as I attended grade school. In fact, I was to be steered to a vocational school and not consider university or higher learning.

This forecast seemed to dog me throughout grade school. Those who had a less than positive outlook on my educational future pointed to the fact that I wouldn't close the letters a, o, or p when handwriting. They tested my eyes and found no issue, so they concluded that it was a learning issue, meaning I would never read well and thus not get far in school. Little did they know, I would go on to become proficient at reading and writing.

My elementary school highlights include my first kiss from a female who wasn't a relative. They also include my music classes. I exceled in them, which couldn't be said for my other classes. Gym class was fun, too, and I always looked forward to joining in, although I never rose to the top of athletics in any school.

Over the years, our family moved often. I spent each year of junior high in a different school. For Grade Nine, I went to H.A Grey School in Edmonton. I could write an entire chapter about the many good and bad events took place there. The final story about this school, however, is so fantastic that no one could have seen it coming.

My transition from Grade Eight to Grade Nine was dramatic. When I was in Grade Nine, I quickly found out what the real world was all about. Sadly, prostitution and pornography were rampant. I witnessed attractive girls selling themselves in hallways of the school, and a classmate showed me his schedule for visiting older women; he was a prostitute and was only fourteen years old. I heard stories of teachers inappropriately engaging in sexual relationships with students. I witnessed terrible gang fights with weapons that saw the police frequent the school. Drugs were everywhere, and I often saw exchanges of money and drugs. As a young teen, I was uncertain if I should report all these goings on to my parents. I was fascinated by it all, so I didn't tell them what was happening. They did instill in me an godly ethic, though, that prevented me from participating in it. I avoided doing anything I would regret in years to come.

In fact, I had an "I Love Jesus" button on my jacket and kids knew I wouldn't join in on their practices. Some students were reviled and made fun of by others, but they left me alone because I was a musician. My nickname was Libby, which was short for Liberace, the famed pianist. My skill opened doors for me to play for school events and to have the respect of my teachers. This played in my favor since I had been labeled as incapable of attaining a high academic standing. At this school most students weren't expected to accomplish much scholastically.

I was so glad to move on to high school and hopefully be free of the darkness and negative perception of my educational future.

Years later, the Bible college I attended bought that junior high school and moved in. This was remarkable, proving to me that God can redeem any situation no matter how horrible it is. As I walked the halls of Vanguard College, I remembered the rooms and hallways where awful events had once happened. I couldn't help but praise God out loud.

A highlight of attending Queen Elizabeth Composite High School was having Henry Kalke as one of my teachers. He was the proverbial flower child of the 60s, and also a strong Christian who had a wonderful influence on his students. He facilitated the One Way Club, a place for students who wanted to consider spiritual matters. It was there that I rededicated my life to Jesus. I am forever indebted to Mr. Kalke for caring for more than the physical side of his students. I gained lifetime friends in this group, including, Dorothy, Cheryl, and Gary, who I'll talk about in detail in Chapter Seven.

High school was a mixed bag of laughs and tears. There still wasn't much expectation for me to succeed. My music class was great, but the core classes were a challenge. Instead of matriculating to qualify for university, I took the courses that would simply get me a high school diploma.

I also tried my hand at football. I made the freshmen team and was scheduled to play linebacker and tight end. When the first game of the season came, we won—to our surprise. The joy was short-lived for me. The week after our win, I tripped at practice, fell, and separated my shoulder. I was out for the season, and incidentally we lost the remaining games. I'm confident that our standings weren't a result of me being on the injury list. I wasn't that good.

So my entire football career consisted of one game. Remember, while I enjoyed sports, I was never gifted as an athlete.

One summer between years in high school, I decided to help my dad by fixing a pump organ he'd been given. Dad had a habit of collecting instruments and this one wasn't working right. I thought I could repair it while he was at work one day, so I took off every nail and screw. At the end of the day, I had a paper bag of nails and screws and a pile of wood. Did I know how to put it back together again? No. Dad came home to find his organ pretty much worthless. I don't remember any anger or rage from him, and I don't know what became of all the pieces of that organ.

In his book, my dear dad tells this story differently. He kindly states that it was both of us working on the organ, but I believe it's mercy and grace that caused him to include himself in the ruination of the organ. My dad always had my back. He always thought well of me and loved me even when I messed up.

As I came to the end of grade school, the call of God to serve in ministry was ringing in my heart and mind. The next step was for me to apply to Bible college. Initially, my hope was to go to a college in Washington State, but our family didn't have the means to send me and I didn't make near enough money on my own. Instead of an American college, I applied and was accepted at Northwest Bible College in my hometown of Edmonton. My intention was to be taught Bible and at graduation move into a music ministry position in a church.

I didn't consider becoming a senior or lead pastor. Counselling, leading a congregation, and preaching didn't interest me. My concentration was to lead the music. Little did I know that many years later God would change my thinking. In Chapter Four, I'll share how my about-face took place.

I attended Northwest Bible College but must admit that I was one of the worst students the school had ever seen. It wasn't because of the conclusions educators had come to about me while I was in grade school. The real reason was that I didn't apply myself. I still marvel that I completed three years. The professors were very patient with my inattentiveness. A few years later, I returned to finish a bachelor in theology, but I continue to maintain that the school was gracious in not demanding that I take several courses again. A glance at my transcript reminds me how shameful my first three years of Bible college were.

In my fourth year, I had to take Greek in both semesters. Carole could tell you that I applied myself and studied an average of three hours each day just on this one subject. In both semesters, I earned an A. This proved that I could succeed in further education. In fact, while Carole was typing my papers on an electric typewriter—these were the pre-computer years—she noticed that when I studied Greek, my English improved exponentially.

A distraction I didn't mind were the girls. I had heard that Bible college was also called "bridle college." There were so many girls there, and they were both pretty and Christians, so my focus was rarely on studies. In fact, I had a reputation for chasing girls. It got so bad that I asked ten different girls to be my escort to a banquet, only to be rejected one by one until I reached the tenth. The tenth was a beautiful girl who I think only agreed to go with me out of great sympathy. At the banquet, I heard a fair amount of whispering. Later I was asked how I'd gotten a date with Janine. What could I say? It certainly hadn't been my good looks. I attribute it to persistence more than anything.

The professors were wonderful men and women of God. I fondly remember Rev. Ernie Francis, the president of the college, He said something that I've never forgotten, and which I've also told others. He looked at me in class one day and said, "John, you have the right to be wrong."

I also recognize Dr. Jack Hunka, Dr. George Feller, and Dr. Graydon Giles. Dr. Hunka was instrumental in me being hired as the music pastor at Clareview Church on May 1, 1980. Dr. Giles invited us students to his home to have a Newfie (Newfoundlander) jiggs dinner. Oh how we felt loved.

My father taught at Northwest Bible College. This was wonderful for me. Every year, the student body would sing the Hallelujah chorus, by Handel, at graduation. Teaching this massive work to the students required a weekly rehearsal for months. One week, my father couldn't be at rehearsal, so he asked me to rehearse the student body. What a thrill! I was a senior and had the joy of conducting a choir of more than two hundred people. That year, I also played the piano for graduation. To play the Hallelujah chorus, I needed both hands constantly, so I placed multiple copies on the grand piano so I wouldn't have to turn pages.

One year, my father wasn't teaching, but he played the organ and I played the piano for graduation. In addition to the Hallelujah chorus, we played Thine is the Glory, also written by George Frideric Handel.

At college, I naturally became a part of any music activities, including playing for chapel services and joining the music teams that traveled to churches. There were three teams. I played horn in a quintet called Sounding Brass and played piano for a vocal group.

Edwin Ehrenholz, myself, Bonnie Simmonds (our piano player), Al Pohl, and John Purich.

The Bible college had a hockey team that played in the church league. Games took place on Friday night, so I went and helped the cheering by playing trumpet. The games usually began at 11:15 p.m. and lasted until 1:00 a.m., then we all headed to a pizza restaurant. On Saturday mornings I usually got home at 3:00 a.m. Sometimes I'd have to go to work at Hotel McDonald to start a shift at 7:00 a.m. Those were the days of my youthful strength and drive.

For talent night at Northwest one year, I formed a music group we fondly called The-Last-Minute-Put-Together-Gospel-Band. It proved to be an amazingly talented group of musicians, including John Sweeney, who I'll talk about in more detail later. We won an award for our song, but we agreed that I would take the plaque home. I still have it in a box.

Another group that lasted longer was a trio formed by myself, Mike McIntyre, and Darrell Widmer. I played the piano and the guys sang. We called ourselves Destiny, but at church we were known as Trinity, which was somewhat annoying to us.

The college had many exceptional musicians and gifted people while I attended, including Mike McIntyre, Darrell Widmer, Dave Dutka, John Sweeney, Dwain Peregrym, Greg Johnson, Vern Johnston, Roc Weigl, and many great female singers. When Darrell, Dwain, or Greg sang as soloists in church on the weekends, they would ask me to go with them and play piano. This was another obvious distraction to my studies, but I couldn't resist joining in with the exceptional people who surrounded me.

One weekend, Dwain and I went to a county fair where he was going to sing, and I was going to accompany him on piano. I had stacks of books of songs he liked to sing. Dwain looked at them and said, "You will no longer be using books to play for me." He wasn't being cruel. He was just pushing me to play the songs by heart because I had played them all so many times before. Years later, another friend, Teddy Rogers, did the same. Like Dwain, she said, "The song is in you, so you don't need the book." I'm so grateful to these friends for challenging me to progress in my playing. Their encouragement also moved me toward writing my own songs. Most of the songs I wrote were in collaboration with others, including Carole. Rarely was I inspired to write the lyrics. Carole, our friend Merlyn, and others would present me with lyrics and I would seem to have the inspiration to create the music. I'll go into more detail later.

Somehow I made it through Bible college while continuing to study piano. In total, I took piano lessons for seventeen years. Dad had started me on the journey when I was six years old and was my teacher for a few years. Along the way, my teachers included Mrs. Richardson, Mrs. Upright (no pun intended), Yana Tubinshlak, Beverly Burrows, and Elsie Rempel. Additionally, I had some coaching by incredible artists such as Geron Davis and Stan Whitmire. Their input was both insightful and impactful. Although I had studied long and with illustrious musicians, I never earned a degree in piano. I finished my piano studies by earning a Grade Ten from the Royal Conservatory of Music in Toronto.

No style of playing has been too difficult, although I have always struggled with technique, such as the beautiful runs some can play. My strength has been to accompany and support singers and musicians.

I've played for hundreds of weddings and funerals. After a while, I developed a list of songs that could be used for each. At times, someone will request a new song be added.

One wedding in particular sticks out in my mind. As it was a large wedding, I prepared to play for thirty minutes prior to the ceremony. I had a list that would last long enough. As the hundreds of people found their seats, I noticed that one person was missing at the appointed time: the bride. She wasn't in sight thirty minutes later, and even one hour later. That would have been challenging for any musician, but more so for me, so I began to repeat songs. After playing the songs three or four times, I began to play any song I knew, although of course I played them in a tender, elegant style. The songs that came to my mind were various

Christmas carols, "How Much Is that Doggie in the Window," and the Canadian national anthem. I also asked the crowd if they had any suggestions. I don't recall if I was given an honorarium, but playing for over an hour and a half should have earned more than a handshake.

My musical tastes are distinct and were shaped by my father's attention to a few styles—although we do differ in certain styles that we enjoy. I learned to love quartets at an early age because Dad took me to concerts. I also learned to love black choirs and brass bands. I never really enjoyed country music, although the Oak Ridge Boys have been among my favorites. Even though they have sung country, they are a quartet, so I learned a tolerance and even enjoyment of country music. I bought all their long-play albums and attended concerts whenever they were in Edmonton.

I enjoy music that is both secular and sacred. In the secular field, Chicago, Earth Wind and Fire, and the Bee Gees are my all-time favorite bands, probably because of the horns for the former two and because of the writing skills of the latter. Christian singers and bands I love range from the Gaither Vocal Band, the Archers, and Andrae Crouch to Kirk Franklin, For King and Country, Mercy Me, Love and The Outcome, Zach Williams, and Finding Favor. My varied YouTube playlists show that, for me, value can be found in most styles.

While studying at Winnipeg Bible College in the mid-80s, I happened to hear a long-play record of the Brooklyn Tabernacle Choir. It was wonderful. Little did I know that Carole and I would sing in the choir as a part of a seminar we attended there. That choir is still a favorite. Thirty years later, I have many more of their albums, but now they are on CD. We've been to that church numerous times to attend seminars for music and for pastors. What a thrilling place to be for exceptional Christian choral music, as well as to hear the Word of God and pray with zealous believers.

While a member of the All City Symphonic Orchestra,
it was a great experience to play a concert in Jubilee auditorium.

In high school, I became quite proficient at playing the euphonium. In my sophomore year, I auditioned for an elite orchestra of high school students, the All City Symphonic Orchestra. While my tone was superior, my technique wasn't as strong as the candidate I was in competition with. His tone was lacking, though, so we were even. The conductor took us both with the hopes of seeing us improve in the areas where we were weak. The orchestra included 90 students playing strings, woodwinds, percussion, and brass. We travelled to Great Britain where we played in Cardiff Castle, Alexandria Hall, and the Royal Albert Hall. I may not have been targeted for scholastic excellence, but this experience showed that there was more to me than my teachers supposed.

One event that will forever be emblazoned on my mind is playing in Cardiff Castle with orchestras from four countries. We played the 1812 Overture by Tchaikovsky, with cannons going off on the hills outside the castle, as well as fireworks. It was dark and raining, but what an experience. I could barely get the air to play. It was overwhelming in its beauty and sheer grandeur.

We had two performance suits, depending on the occasion. This was our formal.

After the performance, I somehow got separated from the rest of the orchestra. There I was, walking down the road with music and horn in hand, with the rain beating down. Suddenly, a black limousine stopped beside me. The driver got out and asked if I wanted a ride.

"Sure," I said. "But who is in the car?"

He told me that it was none other than the Minister for Culture and Tourism of Wales. Apparently, he had been at the performance and stopped the car to help a young Canadian in need. They drove me to my dorm at the university, giving me another story to add to this mind-boggling event.

Music must have been an inherited activity for me. My father had surrounded me with music, modeling musicianship and always encouraging me. So it's no surprised that I was stirred to take up so many instruments. Studying music has always been a solace for me.

While living in Singapore many years later, I was inspired to learn to play guitar. This was one instrument I had no clue to play, although I had owned a guitar while attending Northwest Bible College. My father never played the guitar, either.

I started by going online and working on playing open chords. The only times I played the guitar was during family devotions, so that we would have accompaniment when we sang worship. I was limited by my experience and knowledge.

Later, when we needed money, I sold the Takamine guitar I had bought in Singapore. It really hurt to let it go. Not long after, though, my nephew Jared sold me his Epiphone guitar. I may never be proficient as a guitarist, but I'm satisfied just to play for our devotions. If I had been smart, I would take advantage of all the many wonderful guitar players I've known and learn from them, not the least of which is my own son, Jeremy.

Let's return to the days when I attended Northwest Bible College. I had to take a bus from Mom and Dad's house, which took close to forty-five minutes. One day I was so tired that I fell asleep and missed my stop, resulting in me missing a class. I surmised that getting a car would solve the problem. A friend of mine had a truck, two cars, and a motorcycle, so he asked me if I wanted one of his cars. "Of course," I said, not realizing I would need money for the gas, upkeep, and insurance. Nevertheless, I had my first car. It was a '67 Buick Riveria with a huge 430-cubic-inch engine. That sounds great, but it had body damage, guzzled oil, and had accumulated many miles. Still, it was my car.

On the way home one day, in a snowstorm, I was hit head-on by a truck. The car was destroyed. Since the car was large and I'd had my seatbelt on, I wasn't physically injured. The accident happened in front of my aunt and uncle's home.

When Aunt Doris came running out to see what had happened, she found that it was her nephew in the accident. She comforted me. I was more disturbed than injured.

During my three years at Northwest Bible College, I had two other cars. My Chevy Vega was also in a head-on collision that wasn't my fault. The other driver had gotten into his car, very angry, and came screeching out of an alley as I was passing. He hit me dead on. My car still worked, but the hood was bent and it couldn't open. That car guzzled oil, so losing it wasn't a huge lose.

Then there was my Ford Tempo. It was a tank and had dints everywhere, including in the passenger door. That had happened when a woman in the right lane next to me had decided to turn into me at a light. A police officer had seen her crazy move and asked her, "What were you thinking"? Her response still rings in my ears. Pointing to the left, she said, "I wanted to go that way." The officer looked at me, I looked at him, and we wondered how she had ever earned her driver's license. At least the Tempo got me to school and home again.

Except for one day when I was running out of gas and had no money. As the gas needle was going over the empty line, I began to pray. I was far from home. Just as I asked God for money to get gas, I slowed to turn right and got rear-ended. The guy who'd hit me noticed that the car had so much damage, so he apologized and offered me $20 dollars. I agreed, filled my tank, and went home.

My years at Northwest were an adventure to say the least. From 1977 to 1980, I was in ten different accidents. Only one was my fault. I was slowing down for a light and thought I saw a friend to my left. Distracted, I misjudged the distance between me and the car in front of me and rear-ended it. Unfortunately, it caused a chain reaction.

Although car accidents have become less frequent for me, Carole has had memorable accidents, too. Not wanting to embarrass her, I'll share just one. One day, as I was studying at home, I heard a boom outside. It was so loud that it shook the building. I wondered if a war had broken out! When I opened the door, I saw Carole sitting in the car with a shocked look. Somehow her car had crashed through the fence and hit the house.

They say that most accidents happen near your home. That would be accurate in our case.

Gladly, Carole was alright. The car had some body damage, but I wasn't concerned about that. Like Jeremy, Carole is a very good driver. This one incident wasn't indicative of her skill and attentiveness behind the wheel. In the many years I've known her, she's far fewer accidents than I have.

Bible college brought me more than knowledge of the Bible. I built many friendships and got my direction for the future. In addition to grade school, Bible college, and studying music, I went to seminary and earned a master's degree and doctorate to serve as effectively as I could.

The years Carole and I studied at Providence College and Theological Seminary, formerly known as Winnipeg Bible College and Seminary, were enriching and very special for us. In total, we studied there for eight years. We made many friends there among the students and professors. Suffice it to say, the school was a place of discovery and growth, but it was equally a safe place to learn because of the people who served as staff and professors. We learned about the Bible, as well as about ourselves and our marriage. The school is very special to both of us for what it did to help us grow as Christians and as husband and wife.

At Providence, we witnessed weather, some may say, of biblical proportions. Two winters and one summer stand out in my mind. The first was the winter of 1988, which I will never forget. On a Friday that looked like any other, snow began in the late afternoon. I was in the office of my friend, Dr. Henry Schellenberg, when the news came that a snowstorm was on its way. I looked out the window and didn't believe the forecast, but within an hour it started to snow and didn't stop for days.

While studying, we lived at Providence House, an apartment building for married couples. It was a ten-minute walk from the school. We went home that Friday, and on Saturday morning the snow was so high that we couldn't leave the apartment—and it was still falling. Two brave souls forced the front door open and put on cross-country skis on but couldn't get out of the parking lot.

We later found out that the snow was so high in Winnipeg, forty-five minutes to the north, that tanks were used to move essential service personnel around the city.

On Sunday, no one could possibly get to church, so we had a church service in our building's common room. One student preached, another led worship with his guitar, and a couple held a Sunday school class for all the children. We couldn't get to the store, so we all shared groceries to get through the cold disaster.

The following summer was the hottest I've ever experienced. I have lived in Singapore, which is just one and a half degrees north of the equator. It's hot in Singapore, but the temperature in southern Manitoba that summer was often in the mid-40s Celsius.[18] Carole was working in a cool office, but baby Jeremy and

---

[18] For our American friends, that's roughly 111 degree Fahrenheit.

I had to endure without an air conditioner. Jeremy made it through, but I ended up in the hospital with heat exhaustion.

It was twenty-three girls and me. Notice that my hair is a mess.

During the summers between school terms, I looked for jobs. One summer I was hired as the musical director of a girls choir, the Treble Teens, a well-known community choir that did television commercials and had performed around the world. Sadly, the choir disbanded one year after I was hired, due to financial constraints. Imagine working with twenty-five teenage girls! It was an experience I won't soon forget.

In my final year of studying for my Doctorate of Ministry, I had a January class. I got to the school one evening and unpacked in my dorm room. I quickly looked out my window and then turned in. The next morning, I woke up to a snow dump that reminded me of the one in 1988. Paths had to be cut through five-foot drifts for people to get to the student center and main building. Southern Manitoba can experience extremes in weather that would challenge even the toughest person. The first day of class was cancelled, since professors couldn't get to the school.

Providence was a wonderful place to grow as a person, but I admit that one year I was struggling internally. Carole ended up going to church alone while I sulked in a deep depression at home. She attended a wonderful church, the St. Pierre Bible Church, where many of the students attended. Eventually, I went with her and the depression lifted. Carole has always been such a stabilizing force in my life. In the next chapter, we'll turn to gaze upon the woman I love.

Chapter Four
CAROLE LYNNE TELMAN

What a beauty.

The story of how my life has intersected with Carole's is remarkable, one that some just can't believe.

To best understand how amazing our relationship and marriage is, we must go back to when I was a young child. Unknown to me, my Sunday school teacher as a young child was none other than Carole's grandmother, Eileen Wicks. In addition, Carole's parents and my parents were friends. As I mentioned in Chapter Two, my parents and Carole's attended the Salvation Army corps in Edmonton.

On our first date, I asked Carole if she was any relation to Wayne Wicks. Wayne was an excellent musician who played euphonium in the band my dad conducted. She told me that Wayne was her uncle, and from there we connected the dots.

There are interesting parallels with our families. Carole's Uncle Ron and Aunt Trixie were married the same day my parents were married in 1958. Both Carole's parents and mine had a miniature black poodle, and they also had the same china.

The one major difference between the Wicks and Telman families, however, was the way we conversed. The Telmans are loud and all talk at the same time (remarkably, we still hear each other). The Wicks family is quiet and docile. They talk one at a time and wait patiently to speak.

Carole and I had to learn to forge our own way of navigating communication. The first time Carole experienced a Telman get-together, she had to excuse herself, step outside, and weep. It was emotionally challenging to her.

When I first saw Carole, it was at church where I served as music pastor and she was wearing a long green dress. After the service, all of us younger folk went to someone's home, which is where I met her and felt a spark. Not only was she attractive, but I noticed that she was *all in*. She didn't just go to church like other girls. She worshipped, went to prayer meetings, and brought her Bible with her.

I'll never forget when she auditioned for the choir. I played the piano and she sang Amazing Grace. Honestly, I don't know if it was her beautiful voice or her physical beauty, but I was hooked. She wore a white blouse and a black tube skirt and my heart was beating fast. How could such an attractive girl be such an incredible singer, and a strong Christian to boot? I had found the one I wanted to spend my life with.

In his book, my father wrote,

> John met a lovely girl by the name of Carole Wicks. She was one of his parishioners at Clareview (Church) where John was serving as music director. At first it didn't seem to catch but Carole's mother, Edith, was convinced that they were meant for each other.[19]

He was correct. Carole wasn't all that interested in me, but her mother saw something that she felt was worth encouraging. I received invitations to the Wicks home only to have Carole tell her parents, "You host him. I have to

---

[19] Telman, *A Laugh and a Tear*, 248.

study." This frustrated her mother, but Edith Wicks has a stubborn streak. She doesn't easily give up when she believes something is good for her daughter. Once Carole decided to date, it didn't take long for us to realize that our future would be together.

She was studying medical transcription at the Northern Alberta Institute of Technology. I wanted to be with her, so I picked her up early in the morning and drove her to school in my car. I learned that she liked a certain kind of gum, so I would leave a package of it on her seat when I arrived to get her.

When Carole and I were falling in love, we use to send each other love letters. They were written on paper. We now store those cherished love letters from the early 80s. Carole wrote her notes on fancy paper and put them in fancy envelopes.

One of the fun things we did, some which our pre-marriage counselling encouraged, was to go somewhere private and each take five minutes to talk and then five minutes to listen. We were to focus on the eyes of the person speaking. We did this several times and it really helped us to become attentive to each other. It may have strengthened our relationship from the beginning.

It took less than a year for us to tie the knot, but when we did it was for a lifetime. Dad wrote the following regarding the wedding: "It was an event which we will never forget, and we gained another most precious daughter. We were happy to become related to the Wicks family."[20]

Our wedding party from left to right: my sister Melody, Carole's sister Valerie, Carole's friend, Alice, Carole, myself, my friend, John, my friend Darrell and Carole's brother Mark.

---

[20] Ibid., 254.

At our wedding, we had a brass band consisting of our fathers, uncles, and friends, and it was conducted by Carole's Uncle Wayne. Our mothers and aunts also sang. It was a most amazing way to celebrate.

Aunts and friends serenaded us with song.

To celebrate our honeymoon, we went to a cabin in Saskatchewan that Carole's grandfather owned. Unfortunately, the weather was rainy and cold, so we couldn't spend time on the beach and the seasonal stores were closed. There really wasn't much to do but play cards and talk, so we went to our new apartment sooner than we expected.

Carole became very sick on our wedding night, complicating things. I remember her saying, "I can't breathe." I told her to breathe, but she insisted in frustration that she couldn't. An ambulance was called, and I followed in our car.

A funny thing happened while I waited, by her bed, for the doctor to come. I fell asleep and dreamt that the doctor came in and said that it wasn't appendicitis. In my dream, he was Asian but spoke with a New York accent.

Then a hand touched my shoulder and woke me from my slumber. You may not believe this, but it was the doctor in my dream and he was Asian. He told me that it wasn't appendicitis, not with a New York accent but with a Canadian accent. We decided that it may have been an allergic reaction to all the many flowers at the wedding. Carole recovered, and we started on our journey as husband and wife.

We were married for seven years before we adopted Jeremy, and those seven years allowed us to grow close before facing the challenges of parenting. Carole so enjoyed being a mom. I saw evidence of this in the creative work that she and her three-year-old posted on the fridge and walls in our new home in Kansas City, where we soon moved.

Most people who knows Carole can see that she is balanced, steady, and dependable, but one time she showed that she also has a fun, mischievous side. It was a Tuesday evening after rehearsal at church when I came home to find Jeremy and Carole gone. I went up to Jeremy's room, turned the light on, and stepped inside. What I didn't know was that Carole and Jeremy were hiding behind his door. They jumped out and totally surprised me. This was so out of character for Carole. Jeremy loved that his mom was so much fun.

At one point, our family was down to one car. We fussed initially because of the inconvenience caused by driving back and forth between summer school and work. Fortunately, it didn't take long for us to see an advantage to this arrangement. Every morning, we were together for devotions—mom, dad, and son. It was great, but we never could have imagined just how great it would turn out to be!

As we prepared to leave the house one special Thursday morning, Carole took a moment to seek the Lord's direction for a devotional reading. She felt prompted to go to the bookcase, where her eyes rested on a book of encouragement for stressful times, called *Who Put the Skunk in the Trunk*.[21] She pulled it off the shelf and we started reading it.

We enjoyed the first chapter that morning. Peppered with humorous anecdotes, its theme was "priorities." At the end of the chapter, there was a list of quotes and quips that were both humorous and thought-provoking. However, the last quote caught us a bit off-guard. It was a poem about cancer and the limited power it has in a person's life. We couldn't quite make the connection between the contents of the chapter we had just read and the poem.

I knew of someone whose mother was ill with cancer. It occurred to me that a copy of this poem might be just what he needed.[22] That was my thought. However, God had other plans!

Later that morning, while I was getting ready to leave my office at church, one of the counselling pastors, Randy Burns, stepped in to ask about an unrelated matter. Immediately I felt compelled to read the poem to him. Both of us were in a rush to get somewhere, so I grabbed the book and read it to him as we hurried

---

[21] Phil Callaway, *Who Put the Skunk in the Trunk?* (Sisters, OR: Multnomah Press, 1999).

[22] Due to copyright issues, we are not able to provide the poem here.

down the hallway. When I finished, Pastor Randy exclaimed, "John, this is God! Let me make a quick copy of that." We quickly ran the copy of it and went our separate ways.

Unbelievably, and unknown to me, it turned out that Pastor Randy was on his way to meet with a family who was about to receive bad news about their father: he had cancer. Arriving at the medical office moments before the doctor was to speak to them, Pastor Randy was armed with encouragement.

"You will not believe how much God loves you," he told the family.

I had received that devotional, *Who Put the Skunk in the Trunk?*, two years previous while going through a hard time. As a family, we had started reading it then, but for some unexplainable reason we had put it aside before finishing. The Thursday morning when Carole pulled it off the bookshelf, the bookmark was still where it had been placed two years ago.

This certainly proves that God loves people. He knows what lies ahead of us. Time, circumstances, and distance don't limit God. This truth is for you! God loves people.

Our devotional life has often strengthened and empowered us individually and as a family. Sadly, we haven't always set aside time to have devotions together. I'm ashamed to say that Carole and I didn't start having devotions on a regular basis until we had been married for more than twenty years. I would never recommend this to couples. Spending time together with devotions is one of the most important disciplines a married couple should nurture and maintain.

We began in earnest to have devotions together shortly before moving to Singapore. Our apartment there had two bedrooms, and since there were only two of us, we dedicated the spare bedroom for prayer, worship, and reading scripture. On the four walls, we hung pictures of people we prayed for every day. Some days, we prayed for Michael Jackson, Donald Trump, Mylie Cyrus, Britney Spears, O.J. Simpson, and other celebrities. Other days we prayed for people such as Mark Zuckerberg, Ray Romano, Elton John, Justin Trudeau, and Pamela Anderson. We prayed, and continue to pray, for the salvation of celebrities, but we also prayed for people we knew and for entire countries. Maps were also hung on the walls.

The apartment was furnished with two sets of kitchen tables and chairs, so we put one set in the devotional room. On the table we spread papers of requests people had written for us. We also laid down our Bibles and lyrics to certain songs. My guitar was also in the room, so we could worship as a part of our devotions. After praying, we would read together from a stack of God-centered scriptures written out on index cards. Here is one example: *"You, O Lord... are my refuge, my portion in the land of the living"* (Psalm 142:5). This was a wonderful place and a wonderful time for us. I believe important business was done in that room.

Carole usually read scripture systematically and kept track of the different prayer lists we had for each day. In recent years, she has created a spreadsheet so that even if we are separated by location, we can get on Skype and remember people and situations in prayer.

Do you sometimes wonder about how your prayers are answered? There are many different ways in which God can answer prayer, but we decided that our part was just to faithfully pray and not worry about the answers. It seems that some people, when they don't see answers, quit praying. We prayed for Michael Jackson, and he died. We don't know what happened because of our prayers for him, but it doesn't matter to us. We just pray and leave the answers up to God.

We have also prayed for the churches where we've served. We seek God's blessing on our congregations and for the wonderful people we've had the honor to serve. Though we've moved on for many churches, our love and care for those congregations hasn't diminished.

At times God has placed it on our minds to pray for someone we don't regularly include. One day while we were driving down a highway, God impressed on my mind to pray for Tris Imboden, who plays the drums for the Grammy-winning band Chicago. We've never met him and know very little about him, but that isn't important. What's important is being obedient to what God lays on your heart.

Carole has lovingly endured things that for others would be annoyances, including my nocturnal dream life. Many nights she'd had to catch me before I sleepwalked down the street. Additionally, there are times when I've suddenly jumped out of bed to wrestle lions, tigers, and bears. Oh my! The dreams are so vivid to me, including songs and colors. Carole has put up with a lot in our marriage, but this is a different kind of frustration. She has been so gentle with me and has never complained.

She isn't totally innocent when it comes to interrupting sleep, though. One night in Singapore I was sleeping soundly when I was awoken by her. She wasn't sleepwalking or snoring; she was speaking in tongues. I knew she wasn't awake, so with a great deal of fascination I rested on my elbow and watched. In the morning, she told me that she had been in a spiritual battle in her dream. Wow.

It seems like sleeping is as eventful as our waking hours. One night, we were peacefully sleeping when Carole shrieked. I jumped out of bed, not knowing what had happened. Was it a nightmare? No. A bat had somehow gotten into our bedroom through a heating duct. Since we'd closed our bedroom door, it was flying around trying to find a way out. Carole continued to scream, causing me to move so quickly that I pulled my hamstring. I was hopping around, trying to avoid the bat while Carole screamed. It must have sounded scary to our neighbors.

Somehow we got out of the room and closed the door. We heard the bat continuing to fly around the room. We quickly got our jackets on and went to Carole's parents' home. There was no way we would stay another night in that apartment. Before that incident, we'd heard scratches in the wall and wondered if the building was infested with bats, mice, or worse, rats. It was a challenge to sneak back in later and take all our things out, but we did it and didn't look back.

Our tastes in music,[23] food, and television shows are very similar, so we don't argue over what to listen to, eat, or watch. One of the practices we've entrenched in our lives together is to go to bed happy. This is done in two stages First, we watch an old sitcom. For example, we'll bring out a DVD of *The Andy Griffith Show* or *The Dick Van Dyke Show* and watch an episode. Then we typically read for a while. This promotes a restful night's sleep. It also deepens our relationship in that we set aside time together in the evening, as well as in the morning, when we have our devotional time.

Carole and I have always been dog lovers. We had wonderful experiences with dogs as children. Mickey was our dog when I was growing up, and Carole's family had a black poodle named Mitzi.

When Carole and I bought our first house, we also bought a beautiful Lab-Rottweiler mix that we named Bernie. She was a beautiful dog who spent most of her time in our large, fenced-in backyard, but she would suddenly show up at the patio door when Carole was about to feed her. She played with Jeremy and protected our property from the many animals that came out of the forest. One evening, Bernie cornered an opossum in the corner of the yard. It was hissing and could have attacked Bernie, so we took her inside.

One very sad day, we found Bernie unconscious. The vet told us that an autopsy would be expensive, so we decided not to find out what had killed Bernie. There were no visible marks of a bite, so we wondered if she had been poisoned.

---

[23] Where we differ is that Carole loves Blue Grass Music and I'm not a fan of that musical style.

Not long after losing Bernie, we adopted Pepper, a street dog we found at the pound. Pepper wasn't house-trained and did his best to make our house his bathroom. He was a grey-black poodle who didn't like to be cooped up in the house, or even in our large yard.

No matter what we did, Pepper was a free spirit. In the back yard, we had a very nice dog run where we would put Pepper while we were away, so he could be outside and yet secure. This wasn't enough for Pepper. He tried to squeeze between the chain-link posts and ended up choking himself to death. Carole called me screaming when she came home to find Pepper dead. It was so sad. Although we didn't have Pepper for long, we were terribly shaken by finding him this way.

Before leaving Kansas City, we adopted two sister puppies, Cassie and Nickie, that Jeremy enjoyed playing with. Cassie was an alpha dog and acted like the boss over her sister. Carole thoroughly enjoyed them, especially when she observed Cassie's ways. When Carole scolded Cassie for something, Cassie would nip at Nickie. It was her way of deflecting her complicity in a problem.

Someday Carole wants to have a dog as a part of the family again. Who knows? Maybe we will. I wouldn't argue against getting a small dog. The problem is that we need an animal that doesn't shed. Both Carole and I have long battled allergy problems. A poodle is the obvious choice, but we will have to see. We also have never had a lot of discretionary funds, so the decision will be a careful one.

One day, I was at the office when Carole called. "There's an animal sticking its paw through the attic fan!" she screamed. "Come home now."

When I arrived, the animal had gone, but Carole wanted me to do something about this intruder. I told my friend, David Fine, about the problem and he came over to help up a trap in the attic. While I climbed the ladder, Dave handed me the trap and I placed it in the attic. I crawled into the attic. I didn't see any animal.

Suddenly, I fell through the ceiling into the bedroom closet. Apparently I had stepped right through drywall. All of our clothes were covered in pink insulation.

"Go and have an ice-cold shower right now," he said.

My arm had come crashing down on the counter above the clothes, and I was a mess, but I got into the shower.

In addition to needing to get the clothes cleaned, I had to repair the breach in our closet so that the animal wouldn't have a huge opening to get through, frightening and threatening Carole. That was one Friday I would rather forget about, but the lesson for me was to be awfully careful when attempting any solution.

*Wherever we served, it didn't take long before Carole became a soloist,
as she did here with the choir in Kansas City, Missouri.*

Carole has long been known to be an exceptional singer. What a blessing
that was for me when serving the church in music. I have never been known for
my voice, so she and I made a great team.

Carole is small, but she has that big voice that takes people off guard. She
has always been my favorite singer. It's been difficult for some to accept that she
shifted her ministry to teaching, since she has such amazing talent. Nevertheless,
she was not deterred by the constant requests for her to sing. She knew what
her calling was, and one thing people have learned is that Carole is a strong
person who will not easily bend to pressure. Singing was not to be her ministry
exclusively.

I've accompanied her literally thousands of times to sing in dozens of
churches and at many weddings and funerals, but I will never forget the
time when I played piano as she sang a solo with our choir in front of thirty
thousand pastors at a national conference. She did a wonderful job and made
me so proud.

One of my personal favorite music experiences is when Carole sang "Go
Light Your World" at Christmas Eve services. In a couple of churches, she would
begin singing it with a single candle and the room completely dark. As she sang,
more candles would be light and by the end the room would be emblazoned with
light. Trust me, it was powerful experience.

While serving in Kansas City, she began writing lyrics with a friend, Brenda.
Carole would then give me the lyrics and I would write music. Sometimes the

inspiration came easily, because of the excellent work the girls did, and other times the words would sit on my desk for months.

It didn't take long for a writing group to spontaneously form. Eventually, almost a dozen people showed up at our house with guitars or keyboards. We sang and wrote songs with Nicole and Jeff Hill, who were instrumental in the songs becoming useful to the church.

Carole also wrote a book, *A Portrait of Gratitude*, academic papers, curriculum for studying the Bible, and poetry, including the following:

WITH JESUS IN THE BOAT

It was Jesus' idea to go for a sail
Across the moody waters that day
So why did they think His purpose could fail
And fall into such total dismay?
Alarmed by the storm, they bailed for their lives
Convinced that they could not stay afloat
But there was no danger, no need for despair
With Jesus in the boat
We still hear the call to step in His will
And ride the restless waters with Him
He'll conquer the waves or make it be still
Although it seems our chances look slim
At rest in the storm secure by His side
Convinced that God will keep us afloat
For there is no danger no need for despair
With Jesus in the boat[24]

In our early years of marriage, Carole and I led children's choirs. There was a musical series we performed with numerous children's choirs titled *Psalty the Singing Songbook*. I had to wear a costume that made me look like a giant book. I'll never forget Carole running to cover me one time when I took the costume off. You see, I had no pants on underneath the costume. I had forgotten while standing in front of the children.

One of the musicals, Carole wore a similar costume and played Psaltina. She was such a good sport. After successfully presenting a Psalty children's musical, we shared with the children a cake we had made. The character on the cake was Psalty, and that's how I looked when we did the musical.

---

[24] God's Riches and My Two Cents Worth p. 106-107

We performed many other musicals with children, including The Music Machine, in which I played a conductor, and Sir Oliver's Song, in which I played a giant owl. Playing an owl meant wearing a very large costume with pillows inside that made it unbearably hot under the theater lights. There were other musicals too numerous to mention.

Over the years, Carole assisted me as I led children's choirs, youth choirs, young adult choirs, adult choirs, and worship teams. Her help was invaluable. Not only could she sing very well, but she understood how to work with singers of all ages.

Clareview Church, a congregation of nearly two hundred people, is where Carole and I led an adult choir, young adult choir, youth choir, and two children's choirs. It was said that either you were an usher or sang in a choir. Even the pastor who married us, Pastor Horrill, an Irish tenor, was in the adult choir, and he sang in a children's musical.

Carole has had many jobs that weren't what she desired to do as a vocation. I want to outline a few, which will show that she has a wonderful heart that actively and consistently puts herself last.

She has worked as a medical secretary and has typed as a transcriptionist for numerous jobs. She's not terribly fast, but she is very accurate. Her skill is concentration. She has been complimented for producing precise work.

I have rarely had an adequate salary, so she'd had to work to help meet our obligations. When living in Cranbrook, she couldn't find work that would also allow her to study. She needed a job that was flexible in its hours, so Carole took up a paper route. Eventually, her routes expanded to over five hundred houses. She did this for five years. I couldn't stand to see her so worn by the hours of carrying heavy bags of papers and walking such distances, so I eventually helped her. This was very hard work for two people in their fifties, and we felt it necessary to take two coffee breaks to accomplish this twice-a-week task. It was fun to sit with her and share a bagel and coffee. I believe that this solidified our relationship.[25]

When we moved to Singapore, Carole's help was invaluable. The church we served, Victory Family Centre, had numerous campuses around the island. My responsibility was to oversee the worship ministry, and that meant travelling to different locations each week. In Singapore, you drive on the opposite side of the car and road. In addition, the stick shift of the car I was given was on my left, not on my right. It took a fair amount of work to become accustomed to

---

[25] Later I'll mention one of the problems that resulted from trudging through mounds of snow and trying to keep from falling on ice while delivering newspapers.

this totally different way of driving. Additionally, Singapore isn't constructed in a grid like many cities in North America. The roads were circular, and the signs were of little help.

For this challenge, Carole was the navigator and I was the pilot. We are a great team, but in this instance we were late to church every Sunday for a month. It was stressful when Carole would suddenly tell me to turn right when I was going through an intersection. We laughed about it later, but at the time it wasn't easy.

In addition to Carole's help with our constant travel around the island, she helped me administrate a massive worship ministry. She also helped co-found and administer our website, Truly Worship.

In the previous chapter, I mentioned that the reason I went to Bible college was to prepare to enter the ministry as a music pastor. During the final months of serving in Kansas City, I felt a prompting that there was more for me to do than simply music. I resisted the idea of being the lead pastor of a church, but I resigned myself to pursue this yet unknown ministry I was to engage in. Carole and I accepted the call to serve in music at a church in Singapore, but after a few years we knew for certain that the call from God was for me to serve as a lead pastor.

We had been praying for God to lead us. During a staff meeting at Victory Family Centre in Singapore, the Pastor, Rick Seaward, looked at me and said, "John, I'm afraid we are going to lose you to go and pastor a church." I had never told anyone what Carole and I had been praying about. This confirmed for me that God would be sending us to a church. Where, we didn't know. All we knew was that God wanted me to serve as a lead pastor. Pastor Seaward privately told me that God had told him I was going to leave in an act of obedience to him, so he was to let me go.

One day, while driving to the east side of the island, I had a vision of a white door. It was not imagined. It was literally and physically floating in front of my car as I drove down the highway. The door was opening.

Within two days, I received an email from a church in Cranbrook, back in Canada. They had received my resume from a friend of mine and the board asked if I would be interested in becoming their pastor. This was amazing, since I had no experience as a lead pastor.

Carole and I moved back to Canada and felt that whether it was Cranbrook or not, I would serve as a lead pastor in my home country. We were staying with my parents in Edmonton when Abundant Life Church in Cranbrook flew us there so I could preach and the membership could vote.

Imagine what it was like for us to see the white door of the church. It was the same door that had been in my vision in Singapore. Instantly, Carole and I knew that we would be moving to Cranbrook and serving that congregation and community. Incidentally, we didn't tell the congregation about the vision for several years. We agreed that we didn't want the knowledge of this vision to be used as a heavy-handed leadership weapon. After seven years, we knew it was time for us to pass the leadership on to someone else, but we needed to continue to serve in the lead pastor role.

For as long as I can remember, I had a desire to live in a loft. A pastor friend in Cranbrook asked me if I would like to rent the 1,400-square-foot apartment above the church offices and Sunday School rooms. At last, my dream had come true. The apartment had two bathrooms, two bedrooms, and large picture windows that looked out over the city and mountains. It was very private, as door-knockers didn't know there was an apartment up there, and it was so large that you had to yell to be heard from one end of the apartment to the other.

But we found out just how difficult things could be if we weren't careful. One Friday night, we forgot that we were running a bath. From the back door, which led down to the church, we soon heard a banging. The bath had run over and was pouring down the walls of the church hallways and threatening the pastor's office. The people were so kind and merciful. They even rushed to get a machine that would suck up the flood, since towels couldn't possibly sop it all up.

Living in the loft apartment was a plus for the church, since we could keep an eye out for any potential trouble such as break-ins or vandalism. On occasion, we saw vehicles park in the lot and were suspicious, but nothing negative took place. A few times, the church alarm went off, but when investigated it was a false alarm.

For our next stop on the road of obediently accomplishing what God had called us to do, we accepted the call to serve Ottumwa, Iowa and Hickory Grove Community Church. Both Carole and I were so excited to receive the call to pastor this church and community.[26]

In our lives, Carole and I have been sick or injured many times. Earlier, I mentioned that we delivered newspapers. This went on for years, including spring, summer, fall, and winter weather. Rain was never a major problem, as I recall, but winter was very difficult. First, we had to wear heavy boots and coats in addition to carrying heavy bags of papers. Snow and ice wasn't just a challenge, it was dangerous. We both slipped and fell often and had bruises to show for it.

---

[26] More will be said about Hickory Grove in Chapter Eight.

One Friday, I slipped on the way down some stairs. To brace myself, I extended my arm and snapped my wrist. I screamed and Carole came running. My wrist immediately swelling and I felt extreme pain. Carole, like a good wife, wanted to take me to the hospital, but I said, "Drive me home so I can get ice on it." We still had half a route to finish and it was dusk, but Carole took me home. As I sat on the couch, writhing in pain, she came over to me, put her hand above my wrist, and prayed. We both watched the swelling immediately go down and the pain subside.

Scripture says, *"The effective prayer of a righteous man can accomplish much"* (James 5:16). Let me add that the effective prayer of a righteous wife can accomplish much.

Other healings have taken place in my body that should be told here, since Carole was actively and consistently praying for my health concerns.

My hearing was beginning to become a problem. As Carole and I went for walks, I had to walk on her left since my left ear didn't seem to work properly. Wax buildup wasn't the problem, so I went to my doctor, who happened to be a Muslim. She sent me to a specialist who, after rigorous tests, concluded that I had a serious problem that needed the attention of a surgeon. I drove to Calgary and met with a surgeon who looked at my file and examined me. Then he pronounced what I didn't want to hear: he couldn't help me and I was going to be deaf in that ear. This, of course, was devastating news to a musician like me.

On my way back to Cranbrook, I prayed and told God that I wasn't going to worry. I was going to trust him no matter what the doctors had forecasted. So Carole and I prayed and didn't make much of it.

While in a graduate class on Islam and Current Affairs at Providence Theological Seminary some months later, we decided to sit in the front row so I could hear the professor well. During the lecture, the professor suddenly sounded like he was yelling. It was like the volume had more than doubled. I turned to Carole and whispered, "I can hear." Later, Carole tested my ears and I passed with flying colors.

We returned home, and I went to the specialist for a follow-up appointment. When the nurse called me, she said, "Oh, you're the one who claims a god healed you." She was openly mocking my declaration that God had healed me—until she began the test in a special booth. She stopped the examination, stepped in, and asked if I'd had surgery because my left ear was now not only equal to my right, in some frequencies it was better. The specialist stepped in and asked the same thing, to which I responded with the same answer. He gave me a copy of his report, which stated that I believe I had been healed.

On the way out of the specialist's office, the nurse who had previously mocked me came up to me and asked if I would pray for her family. Obviously, she couldn't explain away what she had seen, so when she had trouble in her life she reached out. Isn't that the way things should be? We witness the truth of God, and people finally understand that God does exist and is our help.

I went back to my Muslim general practitioner with the news that Jesus had healed me. It made sense to me that I'd been healed during a class about Islam, and this gave me a wonderful opportunity to witness to Dr. Kahn. I began to pray for the seed of the gospel, the good news of Jesus, to geminate in her life.

A couple of years later, we saw the professor who had been delivering that lecture at Providence. He asked me if I could still hear normally, and I told him that I could. He confessed that he hadn't believed the healing was genuine but repented of his lack of faith. He was later inspired to believe that God heals.

Another wonderful healing took place some months after slipping on ice and severely tearing my rotator cuff in the right shoulder. It was so painful that if Carole brushed up against it, I would almost pass out in pain. The doctor sent me for an ultrasound, and I almost fell unconscious while being examined. Over the thirty years Carole and I had been married, I had always slept on the left and she on the right. We had to switch, which was no easy task, to protect my shoulder during the night. My arm was almost immobilized. When in a doctor's office later to plan for surgery to repair it, the nurse put a blood pressure cuff on my right arm, and again she had to quickly take it off as I was losing consciousness.

Weeks before the surgery was to take place, I heard the whisper of God say, "Ask." So I quietly did. Instantly I knew that the tear was gone and I was healed. I went to the bathroom to check, and swung my arm around like I was a softball pitcher, with no pain or difficulty. I went back to the living room and said to Carole, "Watch." I dropped to the ground and did pushups. She screamed, "John, don't!"

I went back to my doctor and made movements that were impossible before. The doctor also screamed, "John, don't!" And once again I could witness to her that God had healed me.

The reality of the creator's involvement in our lives is unmistakable. Not only did the doctors see unexplainable changes in my body, but Carole also witnessed the facts of my healings, and she shared them with others.

Not many would know this, but I have broken almost all my toes, some repeatedly. The injuries came on the job, while playing sports, and in accidents around the house. The second toe on my left foot points sideways instead of forward. Six of my toes curl under my feet, and without shoes on I find it difficult to walk. Additionally, when I was a child, I stepped on a rusty spike. It went into my foot but didn't go through. Nevertheless, it was the start of many injuries to my feet. So, if you notice that I'm hesitant to take my shoes off at your home, now you'll understand why. Nevertheless, God saw me through these challenges with the help of a loving wife.

One of my worst problems with sleeping came upon me while living in Kansas City. I could fall asleep easily, and it got to be a problem. I could literally fall asleep while talking to someone. This was dangerous when I was behind the wheel, so my doctor called for a sleep study. Twice I had sleep studies that concluded that I could fall asleep in less than thirty seconds. This was abnormal, since the average individual takes at least seven minutes to fall asleep. Doctors concluded I had narcolepsy, or sleepy brain. It became so severe that I would fall asleep during the day and be awake most of the night. The challenge was to keep me awake during the day, so I was instructed to get as much sunlight as possible. That meant taking medicine and not wearing sunglasses. The medicine was an amphetamine—in street language, speed—and it was very expensive. For a fleeting moment, I thought it might be better to find a drug-dealer who could it sell it to me for less. Don't worry, it wasn't a serious thought. Instead Carole and I went to prayer.

Have you ever known that moment when you knew that you were healed? I did when my shoulder was healed, and I knew the instant my narcolepsy was defeated. Oh, what a wonderful thing to know you are healed! Carole was relieved that I could begin wearing sunglasses again, especially while driving.

Carole walked with me through these and other difficult physical problems with incredible faith and support. Even now, she prays for my eyesight to improve so that glasses won't be necessary.

My personal experiences with healing aren't the only miracles we've witnessed. Carole worked at the Ottawa Civic Hospital, and I was a chaplain there. One day I was called to meet a family that had arrived with their father, who had suffered a massive heart attack and wasn't expected to live.

When I stepped into the hospital, a lady met me and asked if I was Pastor John. I said yes, and she steered me to a corner where she told me more. Her family was waiting in a room close by, so she whispered, "My family told me not to give Dad's money to that preacher." She told me that they were suspicious of all ministers and felt that it was best for me not to go into the room where the family was gathered. I agreed and prayed with her in the hallway. I wasn't allowed to see the man, so I left.

The next day, a Sunday, I told our church about the man, not knowing whether he was still alive. After the service, one of the elders came up to me and told me that God had spoken to him, saying that if I would go with him to the hospital and pray over the man, he would live. I looked outside and saw that it was snowing and cold. I must admit that my flesh wanted to go home, but instead I said, "Okay, let's do it."

The man was barely hanging on, although he was alive. He needed surgery, but the surgeons wouldn't operate because he was too weak. We put on gowns and masks and then were led to where he was. His body was bloated, and he seemed unconscious. The elder told him that we were there to pray and believe that God was going to heal him. We asked him, "Do you believe God can heal you?" My memory tells me that he gently squeezed my finger. We prayed and left after a few short minutes.

I was awakened the next morning by the phone. The woman on the other end of the line was the wife of the man I had prayed with in the hospital hallway, and she was screaming and weeping.

Oh no, I thought. *He died.*

I was wrong.

"He's walking down the hallways without any surgery," the woman said after calming down.

In fact, the surgeons were claiming that he wasn't the same man who had been next to death. When they examined him, his heart showed no signs that it had ever been damaged.

That's not the end of the story. Because of this miracle, the man's sons became believers in Jesus and the family was healed. Additionally, they came to our church and gave their testimony of what God had done for them.

But that's not the end of the story, either. Carole was working in that hospital as a transcriptionist, and she had to type the report about this man. Even though she had to guard confidentiality, she told me that the report had claimed that an unexplainable miracle took place.

Even now, I get chills thinking about how God spoke to that elder. Because we were obedient to go and claim the power of God, physical and spiritual healing took place, transforming a family. All glory to God.

It wasn't a coincidence that Carole typed that report. It entrenched the glory of God in writing but also in our hearts and minds. God is greater than all the trouble we may face.

As time went by, Carole's ministry shifted to teaching. When she was a young girl, she had the desire to become a schoolteacher. We married when she was nineteen years old, and then I took her around the world. Her desire was not fulfilled.

On her birthday in 2014, I told her that we were going to do everything we could for her to earn a PhD and begin to teach. She worked very hard to prepare for the entrance exams. Then she applied to Evangel University, where she was accepted as a PhD student in the Old Testament. How excited I was to see her finally chasing her dreams!

Before she graduated, she was hired as an adjunct faculty member, teaching courses at Horizon College and Seminary in Saskatoon. When she got the email inviting her to teach, we danced around the living room hand in hand.

How that came about is remarkable and reveals the hand of God. We were in Regina, visiting a friend, Tanis, who encouraged Carole to create a curriculum vitae[27] and send it out to Bible colleges. I remember Carole politely responding, "But I only have a Master's degree." Tanis pushed her, so Carole sent her CV to a few schools. One of the first was Horizon College and Seminary. It didn't take long for the academic dean to respond to her favorably. After a couple of interviews, she was hired.

"Thank you, God, for giving us a friend like Tanis who pressed us on to what you knew was going to fulfil your calling for Carole's life," we prayed.

Her first week of teaching at Horizon, a female freshman walked up to her in the cafeteria, told her that she was a great teacher, and gave her a hug. What an excellent start to her teaching career. The confidence that the academic dean had in her also reassured us both.

In addition to music and teaching, she has since ventured into writing. Her first book was a result of a study she did on the thanks offerings of the Old Testament. She also wrote Bible book outlines that are free on our website.[28]

I was so happy for Carole to spread her wings and move into other areas of ministry, but I'm also so happy for those who have benefited and will benefit from her gifts of teaching both in the classroom and through her writing.

After reading this chapter, you may conclude that Carole is the perfect woman. She is not. There are areas where she is weak, but this in no way diminishes the beauty of who she is.

---

[27] A curriculum vitae is much like a resume, but it provides more academic background information.
[28] www.trulyworship.com

Cooking has never been a strong skill of Carole's, but there are times when she has cooked a winner. Early in our marriage, she came across a recipe that we call "Carole's soup." It really isn't soup. It's more like a stew, but it's the tastiest meal you could eat. She fries rice, adds whole tomatoes, carrots, celery, and spices, including basil, oregano, and garlic. Topping it with cheddar cheese makes it a mouth-watering meal. Sure, it's vegetarian, but even the most ardent beefeater would salivate over this dish.

What she does have a passion for is relationships. Her relationship with God was one of the things that attracted me to her. Carole's Bible has been thoroughly marked and diligently studied. Her prayer life has also been a laudable part of her relationship with God. She has dedicated much time to prayer. This relationship has been evident in her dependency on God and stability through all the challenges of life.

Another area where she excels is in her role as a wife. She has held me to live with integrity. Any time she has seen a shadow of selfishness, she has been strong enough to confront me without crushing me.

Our relationship includes laughing together and weeping together. Some people may go days or even weeks without laughing, but Carole and I have daily laughed at what we do or observe. I'm convinced that one of the most important ways to grow a relationship and solidify it is to laugh together. Crying is an equally important way to have a strong relationship. Could many relational troubles be remedied through laughing and crying together? Scripture says so. The apostle Paul wrote, *"Be happy with those who are happy, and weep with those who weep. Live in harmony with each other. Don't be too proud to enjoy the company of ordinary people. And don't think you know it all!"* (Romans 12:15–16, NLT)

In church life, Carole and I laughed over numerous funny things. Most of the time, it was because of something I did, but others also created laughs for us. Let me share a few of the stories. Maybe they'll tickle you, too.

Once, during a church service in Kansas City, I made a huge blunder. Some who know me well might say that I've committed many gaffes, but this one made it difficult to sing a song of worship, "Jesus Is Alive." I didn't have music in front of me, because I knew the song. So I thought. I confused myself by thinking the first chord was the key the song was in. I then played the song in a key that had one and a half thousand people sounding like chipmunks. We had to stop after a courageous try so that the red-faced pianist could play in the correct key.

On another occasion, I totally forgot the song we were going to sing with the choir. We didn't use music, so when the choir director whispered the title to me, "Order My Steps," I tried to recall it. The only thing I could remember was that the piano played the introduction alone. I didn't remember what key it was in, so I began to play a beautiful introduction which seemed to go on and on. I glanced at the other musicians, who had that deer-in-headlights look. I then looked over at the director, and she was mouthing "No" while gently shaking her head back and forth.

Do you want to know how lonely a person can be in a room with more than a thousand people? I didn't know what to do. The church, usually very expressive and vocal, was as quiet as a church mouse. What to do. Then the inspiration came. I stopped and at the top of my lungs I cried, "Does anyone have the music for Order My Steps?" The entire building erupted in laughter. Even the pastor dropped to his knees in a belly laugh. This went on to the point that the choir never did sing that evening.

It was so good to have a friend like Carole to laugh with on the way home. She has a sense of humor that takes you off-guard. I was at work once and noticed that I had forgotten my "brief, the small case that fits inside a larger briefcase. Carole didn't simply bring me what I wanted; she brought a brown paper bag full of my underwear (briefs) and handed it to my assistant. I'm sure glad they were laundered, but it proved to me that this serious woman has a mischievous sense of humor.

Carole is a wonderful example of someone who has successfully nurtured a relationship through the practice of laughing and weeping. There were countless times when she wept with me in prayer, but I know for certain there were times when she wept for me in private prayer. She hasn't just been sympathetic to my pains; she cries out for God to work in her husband's life.

Let this be an encouragement to wives to continuously pray for their husbands.

I wasn't aware that she was actively praying for me for years. Oh, I know we pray for our spouses, but Carole wasn't about to complain about my moodiness and juvenile ways. Instead she prayed, and God answered her. I felt that God helped me to mature and change for the better, and Carole noticed it, too. This isn't to say that I have become the perfect man. Far from it. God did work in my thinking, though. The things I used to value no longer have the same allure. This may have been the point where he began to call me to serve as the lead pastor of a church. I'll always be grateful to Carole, who cared enough to pray.

Being a Canadian by birth, my love for hockey was entrenched into my fall and winter practices. The move to the United States, where hockey isn't as great a priority, was difficult. To remedy the lack of hockey on television, I purchased a huge satellite dish. This was some years prior to the small dish that could sit on a roof.

We were living in a townhouse in Lee's Summit, Missouri. The owner wouldn't allow a dish to be installed in the concrete, so we had to have it fixed to a wood platform and store it in the garage when not in use. When I wanted to watch a game, I had to drag it out and put it in place. To get the signal properly, Carole would be inside at the receiver.

"Is it working?" I'd yell to her.

"No," she called back. "Move it a little."

This process would go on for a little while until I could watch my beloved hockey game. What an amazing trooper Carole was! She had so much patience for my crazy schemes.

After we bought our house, we sold the huge satellite dish, because smaller ones had come into vogue. Now we were ready to watch hockey. What had changed was that I now was more interested in American football and baseball.

I wouldn't begrudge Carole shaking her head at me, but she didn't. Instead she patiently loved me and allowed me my idiosyncrasies, which included painting the outside of our house in February. It was a remarkably warm winter. The daily temperature was often in the 80s Fahrenheit.

Few of the other crazy things I did come to mind, possibly because I'm embarrassed by them. Should more stories be told, you might truly believe I've lost my marbles. But let me assure you that I haven't.

Our house was wonderful, but I felt that renovations were a good idea, so a friend, Steve Box, installed new windows and a second bathroom. Another friend, Troy McCon, installed hardwood floor throughout the house and a marble floor in the bathroom. When all this work was done, the house was truly beautiful, but I wasn't finished.

After a long day, Carole went to bed and I went to work. When she awoke, she was surprised to find that the main bathroom had been renovated. I removed the wallpaper, painted the walls, and then used a sea sponge to give them a textured look. Finally, I outlined the cabinets with seashells. On the walls, I hung nautical pictures. It was stunning. I didn't get much sleep that night, but my crazy ways paid off with a gorgeous bathroom.

Even though I've never been good with tools, it was my home, so I had inspiration to learn home repairs. On days off, and at night while Carole slept, I kept busy with house projects. At one point, the garage door opener needed to be replaced. Instead of hiring a company to do the work, I did it myself, which was a major undertaking for a guy who knew very little about working with tools. You see, my father was never strong with tools, either. Even though his father had been a construction worker, my dad was never trained to hammer a nail or use a screwdriver.

I will never forget one Friday, which was my day off, a day when I typically did the shopping and yardwork while Jeremy was at school and Carole was working at St. Luke's hospital. After mowing the front and back lawns, I took my chainsaw to shape the big bush in our backyard. I set a ladder beside the bush, climbed it, and began to carefully cut the branches. All was going well until I asked myself what time it was. As my watch is always on my left wrist, I took my hand off the saw. The problem was that I didn't release the control in the right hand. Suffice it to say, the chainsaw clipped three of my fingers. Blood started spurting out and I was afraid that I'd lost at least one finger by my foolishness.

I raced in the car to the hospital where the doctors quickly stitched the fingers up. While I was getting attended, Carole came running from her office. A musician losing fingers isn't a good thing, so she was relieved to learn that I would recover the full use of all three fingers. There are scars to this day, but praise God, I didn't permanently damage myself.

The lesson was simple: learn how to work with tools properly and always be safe.

Carole shows patience with me in numerous way, including my love of slurpees—you know, that shaved ice drink. There have been times when I went missing because I was trying to find a store that sold my sweet treat. In hot weather, nothing calls out to me more.

One of our friends in Kansas City had his own ice-making machine at home and I often wondered if that would have been a smart purchase. But Carole had to put her foot down, so you'll find me at the closest 7/11 drinking a Coke slurpee. Lovingly, Carole has also reminded me of all the calories in slurpees, so I've had to curb my appetite for it.

One way Carole and I play together is with a little ball. Some years ago, a ball rolled down the aisle of a church we were attending. Instead of taking it back to the nursery, I tucked it in Carole's purse. She was not to be outdone. Later that same day, I found the ball in my sock drawer. The game was on. Years later, the ball may go missing for a while, but it will eventually show up in the strangest places.

We have driven all over North America. Ten-hour trips are not uncommon for us. To break the monotony, after two hours we'll stop and get a nerf football from the trunk of the car and throw it around in a random parking lot. This helps us from falling asleep. It gives us exercise and another way to have fun together.

On one of our drives from Ontario to Alberta, which was close to thirty hours, we had an interesting experience, to say the least. Our car didn't have air conditioning, so I kept the driver-side window down and kept my left arm on the window as we drove. It was nice and cool while driving on a hot day. When we arrived at our destination, I couldn't move my arm, as it was wind- and sun-burned. It was locked in position and had green sores around the elbow. I was in extreme pain and discomfort, but of course Carole was kind enough to nurse me. The next day, she had to drive as I was suffering from second-degree burns.

We had a Chevy Chevette with a hatchback trunk. Carole helped me load a keyboard into the hatch and stepped back as I closed the lid. The keyboard was too big and the back window shattered in front of our eyes. We were on our way to the church, so instead of explaining the gaffe we drove into the back of the parking lot.

Carole has patiently endured so much with her husband.

Twice I sunburned my back severely. On both occasions, I hadn't worn sunblock when I took my shirt off at the beach. Again, Carole lovingly nursed me by putting medication on my back while scolding me for not being careful.

Another way in which Carole and I have had fun as a couple is through our celebrations. We have always been cognizant of our diet, so we rarely had ice cream in the house, although we both enjoy ice cream.

What a smile!

When something good happens, we recognize the win and celebrate by going out for an ice cream treat. Let me take this moment to encourage you to notice the good things in life and entrench some form of celebrating. Again, this bit of fun will strengthen your relationship with your spouse.

Carole, Jeremy, and myself playing at Disney World.

Playing also extends to all other relationships. Be encouraged to have fun with your spouse. Have fun with your parents. Have fun with your neighbors, and have fun with those you work with. This could be the oil to make the engine of relationships work smoothly. The only caution is that you should make sure the other person equally wants to play.

One day, Carole and I were invited to a friend's house for a barbecue. We arrived early, and I was asked to flip the burgers. While I was busy with this, one of my friends, Don Mootoo, arrived—wearing white pants. Without thinking, I slapped his backside with the flipper, and as he walked away you could see the greasy rectangle. I was horrified by what I'd done. Others had a belly laugh and Carole went to work. She helped the lady of the house by cleaning the pants. Don had to wear something else that day, and I had a flushed face of embarrassment while the white pants hung on the line. Again, I learned that others can laugh at my expense. Sorry Don!

Some people have lost, for some unexplained reason, the ability to laugh. They are easily offended and miss the opportunity to laugh at themselves, situations, and others. This is both sad and dangerous. Laughing at ourselves is a protective measure to keep us from being easily offended. I cannot emphasize enough how important it is to laugh, especially at ourselves. This isn't a way to beat up on ourselves but to judge others as we would judge ourselves.

Believe me, I've made so many mistakes while playing an instrument. There is no greater way to deal with this than to laugh at the mistakes and move on. The key is to observe the quirky and abnormal things that happen every day. There's so much fun around us, if we will only accept it.

Wiser people than me have cried, "Stop being so serious and laugh a little." I'm convinced that our health as a family—my parents, sister and her husband, as well as Carole, Jeremy, and I—can be directly attributed to our desire to find ways to laugh and play every day.

When we were children, we used to ask our parents, "Can we go out and play?" Sadly, people stop playing. The same question could be directed to ourselves each morning: "May I go out and play today?" My hope is that we will all allow this vital part of life to be included in what we do.

Carole and I have tried to be intentional about having a lighthearted approach to life. Sometimes we fail and other times we hurt ourselves with our belly laughs. We firmly believe in the value of laughing, especially at ourselves. Sometimes laughter happens when someone mispronounces a word or misunderstands something. No matter the cause of fun, we are certain that laughing is the best way to deal with most situations. Tears are appropriate at times, but so is laughter.

This is a photo from the "Nut Gallery," proving that we as a family have a unique sense of humor.

My father once told me, "If you get people laughing at you, they're less likely to punch you in the nose." I've taken this bit of wisdom to heart and can say that it works. When people laugh, the tension and angst is lessened. I firmly believe that everyone should find ways to laugh much every day. If it doesn't come naturally through experiences, we should watch a funny show or read a book that has funny stories in it. It's that important.

As a family, we had fun with this pose.

Living around the world has afforded us the pleasure of eating foods that weren't native to our palates. While living in Singapore, Carole tried her hand at another soup-like dish: laksa. Across the street from our apartment was a wet market where she could get fresh seafood to go into this spicy meal. Again, she would present a mealtime delight.

I've learned that she is capable of cooking enjoyable meals, but it isn't her passion. Any weakness Carole may have comes not from her not being able; rather, it's because she doesn't have the interest to spend much time in that area of life.

One obvious difference between Canada, the United States, and Singapore— as well as other Asian countries—is that we would bump into people and they didn't notice. There are people everywhere in Asia. In North America, we like our space. Carole and I noticed this especially when in shopping malls. Saying "Excuse me" in Singapore would be answered with a look that seemed to say, "What do you mean?" People are so used to be jostled in Singapore. Moving as much as we did required that we acclimatize ourselves to the way people thought. That can be challenging but necessary.

In Cranbrook, Carole wore many hats. The church we served was smaller, so she took up multiple tasks. Let me outline a few and show how much of a servant she was—and still is.

Since there were so few people, Carole took care of the computer video. Once a month, she would lead the singing from the hymnbooks that were tucked in the backs of chairs. Additionally, for years she prepared the monthly bulletin. This wasn't a simple job. On the inside covers, she included a calendar with the names of the congregants, so each one would be remembered in prayer at least one day of the month. Additionally, Carole would preach and teach Bible studies for the ladies.

As the church grew and children were added, Carole worked the nursery each Sunday. What impressed me was that this woman, who was a PhD student and blessed with many gifts, humbled herself to get on the floor with young children. My respect for her grew enormously. It takes a special person to be able to teach college classes and to teach in the nursery.

Since we could never have biological children, Carole nevertheless proved to me that she loves children.

Carole has followed me to many places and has patiently endured low salaries and difficult lifestyles, but she has done it with grace, elegance, and without a word of complaint.

With her teaching career now blossoming, I want to affirm her by breaking through any impediments that would discourage her desire to teach. If I need to pay for a flight so she can teach somewhere, I will do it. She has earned my support by her selfless support of me. But even if she hadn't been supportive, she would still need to be honored. She has also earned support by diligently applying herself to her studies. She would get up as early as 5:00 a.m. to read textbooks for hours.

God knew what Adam needed, so he created Eve: *"And the Lord God said, It is not good that the man should be alone; I will make him an help meet for him"* (Genesis 2:18, KJV). This phrase, "help meet," is translated from the Hebrew word *ezer*, which simply means "helper." Carole has been that and so much more. Her help has not been as a slave but as a partner.

So much more could be said about my love, but I will close this chapter with my thanks to God for giving me the best wife I could have hoped for. God knew what I needed in a spouse. I'm certain no one else could have put up with John Telman.

Carole may be small, but she has the strength of a much larger person and her strength comes from her firm belief in who God is. When Solomon wrote, *"The man who finds a wife finds a treasure, and he receives favor from the Lord"* (Proverbs 18:22, NLT), he was talking about John Telman. Anyone who knows Carole knows that this verse is totally accurate. God favored me with the greatest treasure, and her name is Carole Lynne Telman.

John and Carole Telman.

Chapter Five
JEREMY MICHAEL TELMAN

Our son, Jeremy!

What a beautiful child. That was the first thought that came to my mind when I saw Jeremy. Carole and I were taken into a room with a two-way mirror at the Winnipeg Research Hospital to see Jeremy. He couldn't see us, but we could see him. A male nurse brought him into a room and put him on a table. I put my face to the window and shielded my eyes with my hands so no one would see me weeping. This was my son. Carole told me later that her first thought was, *He's so little.* She was concerned a non-infant child like Jeremy, up for adoption, would be larger and harder to handle.

He was perfect.

Baby Jeremy with his new parents, John and Carole.

We went to the doctor's office and saw Jeremy do his patented push-ups. With his blonde hair and beautiful face, we were in love. When asked if we were interested, we said, "Why, yes. We want to be his mom and dad."

At the time, his name wasn't Jeremy Michael Telman. His birth name was Jesse, but with the guidance of professionals we slowly and tenderly called him Jeremy. The significance of this is rooted in the meaning of Jeremiah, a Hebrew name which means "appointed by God." We believed that God had appointed this beautiful person to be our son.

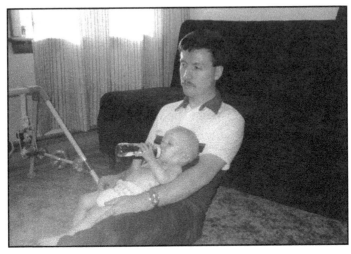

Me and my son.

Looking back over the generations of firstborn Telman males, I noticed that the names of at least four generations began with a "J." Jacobus (translated James) was most popular. My great-grandfather, my grandfather, and my father had all been named Jacobus. Naming our son with a J kept the tradition going.

We'll see if Jeremy continues the tradition—with no pressure on our part.

The prognosis for Jeremy's future was bleak. The doctors cautioned us that he may never walk because of the rigidity in his limbs and that he would probably never hold a pencil. They believed he may have cerebral palsy and would have mental retardation. He had been born eight weeks premature and spent weeks in an incubator without the loving embrace of a mother. The foster parents Jeremy had lived with for the first six months of his life had put him on every prayer chain in Winnipeg. They had spoken healing and God's help over his body each day. They had worked with him until we came along.

Let me interject a fun thing I did when Jeremy was a very young boy. I would lay a blanket on the floor and put him in the center of it. Grabbing each corner, I would swing it around to his delight—and to Carole's horror. She was worried I would drop him, but I never did. He loved it and I got exercise. Jeremy would say, "Dud it agin." As he grew larger, our game discontinued, to Carole's relief.

One night, Jeremy was barely two years old and was fast asleep in his room, but we had a problem that he wasn't aware of. Carole and I were also in our room, but the door wouldn't open. The door handle was stuck, and the apartment was locked. We were concerned that Jeremy might wake with Mom and Dad unavailable for him. At the time, we had no cell phones and no landline in the room, so there was only one way to deal with the problem: I broke the door. You might think I put a shoulder to the door, but that would surely have awoken Jeremy and brought me a fair bit of pain. Instead I put my hands under the door and ripped it apart. Yes, that's right—like a superhero, I pulled the door until Carole, who's a lot smaller, could squeeze out. The story causes us to giggle now, but at the time we were stressed.

As a young child, Jeremy began to learn speech with the typical baby "loidal doidal" sounds, but as he grew he added new words to the English language, like the time "ferteen a clock." Our fun continued when he heard songs we sung but didn't understand what we were singing. For example, when we sang, "Give God the Glory," Jeremy heard, "Give God to Lori."

The evidence that God had overruled the doctors' forecast can be seen by looking at his life.[29] Jeremy not only finished high school, he graduated early. He played soccer, football, and baseball. He is an excellent musician. His proficiency in guitar, bass, and drums is a testament to God's healing virtue. Make no mistake, Jeremy had troubles, but they were not in the areas of intellect and physicality. He struggled in other ways I choose not to highlight. Suffice it to say, there were many tears as he suffered with reactive attachment syndrome, bipolar disorder, and depression.

Jeremy loved his Opa, and his Opa loved him. They could not have been more different, but they truly did love each other.

One summer, Carole, Jeremy, and I attended a worship seminar in the mountains of Colorado. While there, I prayed privately about Jeremy's future. Without Jeremy or Carole knowing, my silent prayer was that God would keep him all the days of his life.

Jeremy was such a beautiful little boy.

---

[29] The story of Jeremy's life and mine have similarities in that both of us weren't expected to accomplish what we have. This is not a tribute to us but to the healing and purposes of God to show his glory over what man says.

God heard my prayer and confirmed it in the most miraculous ways. While sitting in a hall, Jeremy asked me, "Daddy, who is that big man?" He pointed to a place in the room where no one was standing, at least not that I could see. I immediately had the sense that he was seeing an angel, so I asked, "What does he look like?" Jeremy told me that he was very tall and shiny. Something prompted me to ask, "What's his name?" This little boy told me that his name was none other than Keeper. Can you imagine what that did to my heart? My faith in God's care for this beautiful child was strengthened.

Jeremy could be very dark and low, but he could also be so much fun and enjoyable to be around. The emotional swings were hard on him, Carole, myself, and others. Nevertheless, we shared many, many laughs as he grew up in Kansas City. Jeremy could laugh and have fun as much as Carole and I could.

When we moved to Kansas City, Jeremy was three years old. He basically grew up there and it hurt him deeply when we moved away. Our house was comfy, and when we bought it we did renovations, including to his room. One day when he was at school, we tore his room apart and painted it and put in new carpet and window treatments in the colors of his favorite NFL team, the Dallas Cowboys. That was his birthday gift and he loved it, until one year when he suddenly became a Green Bay Packers fan, so we changed the colors, took down the posters, and replaced them with a Brett Favre poster.

One of our Sunday night traditions was to have a snack when we returned from church and watch the football highlights. While Carole prepared the food, I sat on one couch and threw a nerf football into the air above the other couch. Jeremy would run and dive to catch the ball. We both loved this little bit of fun, and he was very talented at this game.

When he played Pop Warner football, he excelled. He had foot speed and a real knack for making tackles and sacking the quarterback. Despite being good at football, though, Jeremy didn't like playing the game, which included hard and physical practices, dirt, and often wet, muddy fields. Knowing what the doctors had said about his future, I always enjoyed watching him run, jump, and prove that God was greater than sickness.

Jeremy also played soccer and was again skilled in running and moving the ball, but sadly he was illegally tackled one day and his knees were damaged. As a teenager, he needed surgery on one knee to repair a torn meniscus. God had healed his body only to be hurt by the reckless play of another player.

One of my favorite memories was American Thanksgiving. While Carole was cooking the turkey, Jeremy and I hung Christmas lights on the house. We were hanging off the roof and having fun father and son time, doing some dangerous things that I'm glad Carole never saw. In the afternoon, we ate the meal and watched football. At dusk, the three of us would go for a long walk and then turn the lights on. I miss those wonderful times that the three of us had together.

When Jeremy was twelve, I felt it would be important to set aside an evening that we would call Father and Son Night. It was usually on Monday. Jeremy and I would go to a baseball game, a movie, or something else he liked to do. Tuesdays were date night for Carole and I, and the two of us would go out for supper and dedicate the time for our marriage.

One date night, we took Carole's car and left mine in the driveway. We told Jeremy we would be home at a certain time, but it turned out that we arrived home earlier. Immediately we noticed that my car was gone. Jeremy was also gone. We were stunned. He had Carole's cell phone, so we called and told him that we would be home early. Then we sat on the stoop and waited. A few minutes later, we saw my car turn the corner and pull up. When we saw his face, it was priceless. It was as though I could read his thoughts: "I'm dead. Dad is going to kill me." It was terribly funny, but I didn't laugh.

After giving me the keys, I told him to go to his room. Carole and I discussed what to do, and then I called the police. I asked if they would mind educating a young man with the legalities of driving without a license and grand theft auto. They said they would come right over.

"Can I ask you to do one more thing for me?" I asked.

"What's that?"

I told them that Jeremy's bedroom was the one over the garage, so he would see a police car with its lights flashing coming up the driveway. They agreed to turn the lights on when they drove up, and they did. I then invited the officer into the living room and brought Jeremy in. The officer was polite as he towered over Jeremy. This was a lesson Jeremy wouldn't soon forget.

Incidentally, some years later I gave Jeremy that very same car as his first vehicle.

So what had led to the car being taken? This sharp young man had noticed his dad's keys. When I was taking a nap one day, Jeremy took the keys to the hardware store across the street and had a copy made. He put my keys back to avoid suspicion, and at the right opportunity he took the car out. Let it never be said that Jeremy couldn't devise a plan.

Looking back now, it was quite funny, but at the time it caused me to be careful where I kept my keys. As a driver, he is responsible and dependable.

When I've had occasion to be in the car as he drives, I feel safe. I'm proud of the person he has become.

In the backyard of the house where Jeremy grew up, we had a trampoline that he enjoyed with friends. I had to avoid it because I ended up needing to go to a chiropractor whenever I got on, but what fun it was for Jeremy and his friends.

Even though he had a rough start to life and wasn't expected to be independent, Jeremy has been a joy to watch. We have witnessed both difficulties and many joys in his life. I studied hard with many teachers to learn music, but Jeremy's ability is truly a natural gift. He didn't take any significant lessons... maybe a lesson here or there from a friend, but Jeremy was gifted and mostly self-taught. He had the passion to learn drums, bass, and the guitar.

Jeremy is a naturally talented musician.

When he was a toddler, he would bang on pots and pans. As a little boy, we bought him a toy drum set. Then, when he was an adolescent, we bought him a second-hand drum set. He had his own studio in the shed, but since it wasn't heated the drums had to come inside, challenging our peace. He played in bands and played for worship in church, which was more significant to us because we knew just how wonderful the healing was that God had performed in his body.

Jeremy's chosen styles of music have often differed from mine, but we have a great respect for each other as musicians. He claims, and is probably correct, that I had promised him piano lessons if he taught me guitar. This hasn't happened yet, but I have a suspicion that if it did, we would both learn quickly.

A few significant physical differences between Jeremy and I include our height, our weight, and our hands. Jeremy is taller than I am and has been for many years. He's slender and I have always struggled with weight. He has long fingers and mine are short and stubby. Watching him play guitar is so enjoyable. He seems to glide along the frets with no effort at all. He's also very competent on the drums and bass. Much like his driving, Jeremy is dependable. He doesn't speed up or slow down like some drummers do. His playing is consistent and easy to follow.

Jeremy in the studio, where he is most comfortable and able to enjoy himself.

When he was a young boy, Jeremy enjoyed rap, so we bought CDs for him, but rap didn't become a permanent style he listened to. He liked the music but didn't rap himself. His musical tastes included music that was too hard for me to listen to, but I didn't begrudge him his likes.

When we moved to Singapore, Jeremy stayed in Canada with friends. It was his choice, and ever since we haven't seen him as much as we'd like to. We haven't often lived in the same city as Jeremy, since he became an adult, so getting together is extra special.

Jeremy and I have had many laughs, including one at a McDonald's restaurant one day. We were rushed, so we pulled into the drive-through. Our intention was to order our breakfast and quickly eat in the car. The voice came over the intercom, welcoming us, and asking, "Do you want a hot fudge Sunday?" We looked at each other and burst into a belly laugh. From then on, all it takes is Jeremy or myself saying the words "Do you want a hot fudge Sunday?" to lighten the mood.

As yet another example of how we had fun, one day we went out for a nice formal dinner with family in Kansas City. Suddenly, he and I decided to take off our socks and shoes and jump in a fountain, striking a Heisman trophy pose.

Jeremy and I at the fountains in the plaza of Kansas City.

Since Jeremy had no siblings, his cousin Jordan became a close friend. They are close in age, and even though they don't see each other often, they truly have a good relationship.

Throughout his life, he has shown such amazing compassion for animals. I thought he might enjoy becoming a veterinarian. The problem with working as an animal doctor, though, would have been that he'd have to see animals suffering, and Jeremy wouldn't handle that well. At times he would defend animals over people. He has always had a righteous anger against those who abuse animals.

Jeremy with his dogs, Nicky and Cassie.

I was in no way a perfect father. In fact, I've often chastised myself for not diligently doing more to be the father Jeremy deserved. But one piece of advice I'll offer here is that fathers would do well to have fun with their children. Aside from board games, children need to see something as simple as a funny face and an invitation to join in jocularity.

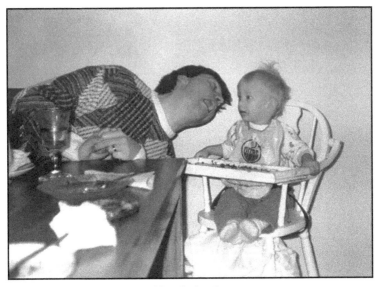

Jeremy found his dad to be a crazy man.

Our home was somewhat of a miracle. Both Carole and I were the eldest in our families and Jeremy was an only child. Ordinarily, this could make for many problems. We did have our share of problems, arguments, anger, and unkind words, but we survived it all and have loved each other by making laughter a part of our home life.

Jeremy's nicknames—he had to have some, after all—were Jer Bud, Buddy, Jer-Bear, and Peanut Head (this last one was fondly coined by our good friend, Dr. Tom Cates). When he was a very young child, he called himself Mimi, but most people just call him Jer.

Earlier I mentioned that Jeremy's name was significant in passing on the tradition of naming the firstborn Telman son with a J. But before he was adopted, his name was Jesse Stanley Thomas Hall. When he turned fourteen, we went out for a deep-dish pizza dinner and I told him that if he wanted, we could legally add his birth names to his name.

"No thank you," he said. "I'm Jeremy Telman."

This deeply impacted Carole and myself. We never kept the truth of his adoption from him, but this told us that he had decided to truly be a Telman.

Jeremy was a handful, but he has this ability to be such a wonderfully loving person. As his parents, our daily prayers have been for God's unmistakable presence to keep him, heal him of all wounds, and strengthen him for his day. God has done miraculous things in his life and we believe that more is coming. The faithful love of God will certainly be seen in his life, just as it has for these many years. I wouldn't be surprised to learn of many more touches of God on Jeremy's life. He was beautiful the first time I saw him in 1989, and he's still beautiful.

Jeremy and his mom and dad.

Chapter Six

MELODY JOY AND BRIAN BIGAM

An addition to our little family came a year after Carole and I were married. My sister Melody married her husband Brian. This was an answer to prayer for our parents, who had truly been concerned she would have no one to care for her. Brian has been that and more. Their story as a couple has been presented in books they have written, but I'd like to share what I've observed.

Not long after Carole and I married, we moved to Ontario. We sold our car to Brian, who had just become engaged to Melody. One day we heard the news that the car caught on fire. Apparently, a piston must have exploded in the engine. I wasn't wealthy enough to refund Brian, but he never complained and didn't hold it against me. My respect for this quiet man began to grow.

Brian, though quiet, went to Bible college and became pastor of a church in Saskatchewan. Melody also graduated and began the journey of serving others. This is amazing, since she could have easily demanded that others help her—but no, she and Brian served.

There is so much to say about this beautiful couple, but I'll try to limit the stories to just a few. Some of what you'll read were terribly funny and others were extremely sad. The truth of the title of this book is most profound when you consider the lives of Brian and Melody. They have experienced many laughs and many tears.

Early in their lives together, Brian and Melody served as children ministry pastors. This makes sense since they are a happy, fun-loving couple that kids were attracted to.

When we're with them, it doesn't take long for us to start laughing, and it won't stop. The most incidental act or word may erupt into uncontrollable laughter. This is one reason we enjoy spending time with them, but they also experience tears. Spending time with Brian and Melody will also result in honest discussion in which they'll always take the affirming stance of patience and encouragement.

One game they play is with their names. They've called themselves George and Judy from Bugsville, Horace and Hilda from Hinton, Larry and Lucille from Leduc, and Delorus and Dilbert from Denver. With all the tears that come, we must find ways to giggle. Brian and Melody have found a way.

Earlier I mentioned that we've all sported nicknames. Brian's has always been Bing. Melody, along with being called Bose, Skootch, Deed, and Bum, has been called Binky. So they are affectionately known as Binky and Bing from Boston. This is another example of playing. It's a simple but fun way that Brian and Melody get us all laughing.

Melody and Brian have always been giving people. They love being with others and show inclusive love to all. One year they took a mission's trip to Guatemala, which is in keeping with their kind hearts. Upon their return, they were shocked to find that Brian's identity had been stolen, which landed him in deep trouble. Evil individuals had attacked this principled man. The result was that Brian had to declare bankruptcy twice. When checking up with them on the phone, Melody didn't talk; she wept. It deeply impacted a brother's heart with compassion.

They moved often since they had very little money to pay rent. Their cupboards and fridge were empty. They had to call on family to even feed themselves. I can't tell you just how hard this was. Tears often flowed in our prayers that God would take them through this deep, dark valley.

At times we would visit our parents and they would be there. Even though we didn't have much, I would often slip a $20 into their shoes. This continued for a few years. On one occasion, I mistook my cousin's shoes for Melody's. Jody didn't know where that blessing came from, but I didn't mind.

Although these were a horrible few years, I saw Brian and Melody live with such grace and godly character. Instead of anger and hatred, they prayed for whoever inflicted such pain on them. Additionally, they have vocally, and with their actions, declared their unwavering trust in God to see them through the fires of trouble.

The Hebrew men in Daniel 3—Hannaiah, Mishael, and Azariah—were in the fiery furnace, but the fire did not kindle on them. You can't go into 7/11 without smelling like smoke, but these three were kept in the middle of a blaze that could have destroyed them.

Brian and Melody, like these young men, were in the hot furnace of trouble, but they came out not even smelling like smoke. God was with them and has honored their trust in him with peace in their lives.

Both Brian and Melody found a place of ministry instead of complaining about being mistreated. The ministry they treasured for years was being chaplains at West Edmonton Mall, which at one time was the largest in the world.

At Northwest Bible College, one of the friends I graduated with, Nelson, had a burden to plant a chapel in the mall. He did, and for decades the chapel was a place where employees and shoppers alike could go to pray and receive counselling. Market Place Chapel was the perfect place for Brian and Melody to serve. In addition to being available to people on a volunteer basis, they visited employees of stores and earned the respect and trust that was needed to help others. They know so many people who frequent West Edmonton Mall, but they also know employees and are patiently accepting of all people. Their time spent there is volunteer, and it takes up most of their average week.

It's hard to imagine two people who smile more than Brian and Melody.

Shortly after I began serving as lead pastor of Abundant Life Church in Cranbrook, I received a call from Edmonton. My parents told me that Melody had two very large blood clots in her lungs and that she was in grave physical condition.

"Please come home now," they said.

I immediately hung the phone up, packed, and left for Edmonton. It was an eight-hour trip, but I probably made it in six. A police officer did stop me for speeding in Edmonton, but truthfully I didn't care. My only sister was in intensive care and hanging on to life.

Earlier, I stated that she and Brian were in trouble financially. When you have very little money to buy food, you buy what you can, which often isn't healthy and promotes weight gain. Melody had put on so much weight and her poor feet were so strained that blood clots had formed, traveling to her lungs. When I arrived, she began to weep and told me she was afraid. So I hugged her and we prayed.

God heard our prayers, and once again she was miraculously healed. After she gained strength, she began to work on losing weight and Brian obtained a good-paying job. Their troubles began to diminish. They talk more about these events in the booklets they freely share with others. Their individual lives and marriage could be described as *a laugh and a tear*.

Brian used to be quiet, but as in Carole's life, the Telman family had an effect on him. Brian learned to talk, and talk loud, like the rest of us. He didn't hold his opinions back. It didn't matter if it was sports, food, or scripture, Brian was no longer hesitant after becoming a part of our family.

Like all of us, they have their own unique ways of enjoying life. Brian and Melody have chosen to visit as many Starbuck coffee shops as they can. Brian once told me that they've visited dozens of Starbucks in numerous cities. This is part of who Brian and Melody are. They are social butterflies. They talk to people and love to be out and about. Their time is rarely taken up watching television. They prefer to visit museums, sit with friends at coffee shops, or visit the elderly. You won't find a more genuine couple who loves people.

This reminds me of Pierre, the young boy I spoke of in Chapter One who came to stay with them when his family was having a hard time. Opportunities to love others seek them out, and that's what you'll witness in the lives of Brian and Melody.

Even our goodbyes are fun.

In 2016, Melody and Brian began a ministry whose name makes total sense to me: 3L Ministries: Love, Live, Laugh. I wish I could chronicle all the loving acts they perform, but their acts of kindness and love aren't intended for the applause of man. They don't look for pats on the back or public affirmation. Their service is first in love and worship of God, then they serve out of gratefulness for the goodness of God. Finally, they serve out of their love for others. They receive no remuneration or support to minister. Instead they serve for the smile of God, and I am convinced that is what they receive.

If you were to check out Melody's Facebook page, you would find many posts of encouragement and love for others. Here's one example from October 6, 2017:

> Never allow challenges to stop you from achieving the dreams or goals you are striving towards. (You can do all things through Christ who strengthens you. Philippians 4:13) I can personally tell everyone God has continually been with me through my life and He has walked with me through all my physical challenges and has guided me through my dreams of going to Bible College and Graduating 4 times, marrying a Pastor and doing Ministry. I am so grateful to God for blessing my life. Doing life and Ministry with Brian has been quite the Adventure and I Love it.

Like us, Brian and Melody couldn't have children, so their hearts were open to share love with many—and they have. They have been extremely giving and inclusive. No one is excluded from their utmost attention and generous kindness. They may not have much money or possessions, but they are rich in other immeasurably ways.

Brian loves books and photography, so between his ever-growing library and looking for that certain shop, he will always be busy and have little time for sports or television.

Whenever Carole and I have occasion to be in Edmonton, we won't have to ask to see them. They will be at my parents' home to spend time with us. Laughs will always accompany their presence, but there have also been times of sober discussion. At times we will stop everything, my father will go to the piano, and we'll sing and pray. Nothing is more precious and profound than taking the time to love, laugh, and live with Brian and Melody Bigam.

Our family, including Brian and Melody, have fun even when we say goodbye to each other. It's been our habit to make the Granny Clampett wave to each other, made famous on the television sitcom *The Beverly Hillbillies.*

We still wave goodbye to each other like Granny Clampett.

If I was to guess who their best friends are, I would venture to guess that it is none other than our parents. They visit Mom and Dad at least twice a week and drive them wherever they need to go. They have also involved Mom and Dad in their ministry of visiting others. On my list of people I love and respect most, they are at the top.

One beautiful couple, Brian and Melody Bigam.

Chapter Seven
FRIENDS

I t may be one of my most defining characteristics that I desire to make friends with everyone. I value friendship and connection with others more than gold.

It is my request that at my funeral, my favorite hymn, "What a Friend We Have in Jesus," be sung. It's words, "All our sins and griefs to bear,"[30] express how God has been a friend to you and me. This is the love of a true friend. The theme of friendship with God is so noticeable in scripture. God is more than a far off potentate we serve. He is near, and most importantly he is a friend to all who welcome him.

Some of our friends do not agree with us on important issues, but we try to maintain a friendship so that we might influence their thinking in a positive way. They may not agree with us with regards to theology or ethics, but we still want them as friends.

Remember, Jesus was called a friend of sinners, and that is precisely what he was. Often those same sinners were changed because of their contact with Jesus. To abandon someone closes the door to communication. It takes intentional effort to remain a friend when someone doesn't think like you do, but it's necessary. Even more than that, it may mean that they have something you need to hear, too.

Carole has noticed that in stores, restaurants, or any place there are people, I attempt to make friends with everyone. In fact, as I'm typing this, I'm sitting in a coffee shop where I have made a friend with a man from Pakistan.

---

[30] Joseph M. Scriven, "What a Friend We Have in Jesus," 1855.

Making friends at times means speaking the little French, German, Spanish, Mandarin, Cantonese, or Tagalog I know. It's amazing how quickly the social ice melts when you attempt to speak to others in their own language. In fact, I have a dream that when I'm retired I will learn languages fluently, then get on a city bus each day with the hopes of telling people about Jesus in their language. This would be my full-time job. I'll get off for a coffee break and lunch but spend eight hours listening to people and attempting to engage them with the gospel by being a friend.

The friendship I value above any other is the one I have with Carole. Carole isn't only my wife, she is my best friend. Over the years, I've been blessed to know wonderful people and to count them as friends. Putting aside some people listed as friends on Facebook, people who in truth may only be acquaintances, I have been blessed to have Carole as my friend. This has been a healing balm when life produced tears.

It would be a mistake not to share just how wonderful a friend Carole has been. Over the many years of marriage, she has laughed with me and wept with and for me. Her stubborn love has driven her to put up with my idiosyncrasies and encourage me when I was low. Carole is not known to have emotional ups and downs. Her consistency has been a wonderful stabilizing force in our home. She is the consummate friend.

DAVID STAM

Dave Stam and I began our friendship in the 1960s.

Over fifty years of friendship.

As a child I had many friends, but one in particular has remained a friend over the decades. David Stam's parents were very close friends of my parents. In fact, his father was a friend of my father when they lived in the Netherlands.

David and I spent a lot of time together playing chess, wrestling, and talking. He has gone on to become a renowned lawyer. His rhetorical ability has resulted in a very successful professional life. He is a kind but strong person who I treasure as one of my first and greatest friends.

H. JOHN KLOOSTER

John and Carole (not Telman).

In 1980, I graduated from Bible college and entered the ministry at Clareview Pentecostal Assembly as the music pastor. This is where I met John Klooster, as he and his family attended the church. Along with his father and mother, he joined the choir. Both of our fathers had lived through World War II in the Netherlands. We also had in common a love for hockey. John played for the church team while I refereed in the "church league."

John became one of my closest friends. Like other friends, John showed such love and care for me. It's hard to put into words just what his friendship has meant to me. He was my best man and trusted counsel in times of struggle.

We used to play racquetball when time permitted. Once while playing, I injured myself badly. If it's possible, I could hurt myself in all situations, and during this racquetball game I broke my ankle and damaged my knee. John has always been sympathetic, but I still remember hearing him giggling over my clumsy play.

Both David Stam and John Klooster, like myself, were born to Dutch fathers. The three of us had so much in common through ethnicity, but we also shared a deep love and devotion to God. I've been so blessed to count the two of them as my friends.

Dave Stam, John Klooster, and I were sons of fathers born and raised in Amsterdam.

Imagine my surprise to get a call from John to hear that he was going to get married and that he wanted me to come to Edmonton to be a groomsman. I was delighted but also amazed to learn that his fiancée's name was Carol. The parallels in our lives were uncanny. The very church where I'd met my wife and led worship was where he'd met his wife and where he would later lead worship. Both John and Carol as well as Carole and myself have served in the ministry. I've preached in the church where John has pastored for many years.

GARY COUET

Gary Couet and I attended Queen Elizabeth Composite High School together in Edmonton. We became friends, which resulted from the One-Way Club I spoke of earlier. Gary and I grew as new believers and were nurtured in our walk with the Lord by Mr. Henry Kalke. I can honestly say that this was a pivotal time in our lives.

Getting reacquainted with Gary and his wife Cheryl
after not seeing each other in decades.

Gary was always kind and giving. I could tell you about his generosity, but I want to protect his privacy. Suffice it to say, he showed great character as we were growing up. He, like other treasured friends, is a gifted listener. Transparency is a strength of his, and he has continued to have the mark of a godly man.

Gary and I lost track of each other for many years, but we reconnected a few years ago. I wasn't surprised that my friend had married a wonderful Christian woman and raised an excellent family.

JOHN SWEENEY

John Sweeney became a friend while we were students in Bible college.

John and I began our Bible college studies at the same time and graduated together. This was no simple accomplishment, considering how poor a student I was. Our class had more than one hundred twenty students on the first day of class, but three years later only a third of that number graduated, including John and myself.

We became fast friends since we were both musicians and found ourselves working together. Like Greg Johnson, Mike McIntyre, Darrell Widmer, and Dwain Peregrym, John and I travelled and provided music in churches throughout Alberta and Saskatchewan. Most of the time, we bunked in people's homes, since we weren't given hotel rooms. John will let you know I snored so loudly that I could have annoyed the dead. In fact, at our wedding reception, John warned Carole what she was in for. I still remember the song he sang at the reception. You see, John knows how to laugh also. He sang "I Will Serve Thee," and said this was our song to each other. Little did he know how accurate he was.

Without spending too much time on him, suffice to say that my admiration for John has always been sky high. I longed to have his ability both as a musician and songwriter. He penned beautiful songs with ease and powerfully performed them.

But that's not why he is a special friend. John is my treasured friend because of the unquestioned affirmation he gave me. He didn't resist correcting me either, but I know his heart and it was fully supportive. Never have I wondered if he was my friend. He is such a trusted friend that he's been a reference when I've had occasion to send my resume to churches. Do you know someone who would fall on a grenade for you? John would be that person for me.

MARVIN DUECK

Marvin and his wife Louise are genuine. I'm so blessed with their friendship.

Marvin Dueck attended Bible college at the same time as I did. We became fast friends, and yet we are very different in several ways. Marvin is quiet and cerebral, although he can have fun. I'm given to impetuous actions. He has served as a counsellor and pastor for many years with steadiness and wisdom. I have been somewhat flighty and quick to move on to the next idea.

Marvin and his wife Louise are the kind of warm people you would first put on your guest list for a get-together. Both are great listeners. They look at you with intentionality. When in conversation with them, you know that you have their undivided attention.

They may dispute this next statement, but I seem to remember going to their home and smelling coffee but never observing them drinking or serving it. When queried, their response was "We like the smell but don't like to drink it." So they brewed coffee but never drank it. Eccentric? It may be different, but their loving character leaves room for grace. Let's just say, I have a giggle when I think of coffee and the Duecks.

One year, they drove all the way to Kansas City from Canada to visit us. This was long before the internet when friends could easily and economically keep in touch. This beautiful couple, if nothing else, is intentional about others.

Terry and Joy have been so warm and kind to me,
you would think I was there brother.

TERRY EDDINGTON

This man is another who, like other friends listed here, has been so kind and loving to me over the years. When I think of Terry, gratitude wells up in my heart. Scripture uses the word "fellowship" in Acts 2:42 as something we should exercise. The Greek word is *koinania*, which means more than having coffee or spending time together. True *koinania* fellowship is about demonstrating self-sacrificial care for others. Terry exemplifies the true meaning of *koinania*.

On numerous occasions, Terry has gone out of his way to help me. One day, my car broke down on the I-70 in Kansas City. With thousands of cars racing by, Terry came to my rescue. This cost him time, money, and effort. He is a giving individual like few I've ever encountered. Terry and his most lovely wife Joy haven't hesitate to host us when we were passing through Kansas City, even when Terry was suffering with a terrible back problem. Few people exhibit such true fellowship.

With sorrow, I recently received a call from Terry's wife Joy and learned that Terry had passed away on January 16, 2019. This hurt me deeply. Joy asked if Carole and I could come to the funeral service and if I could lead in singing. What a wonderful honor that was!

We drove to Kansas City and met with the family prior to the service. The attendance was amazing. Hundreds came, and a number of people publicly spoke in tribute to this friend of mine. Even now, I tear up when I think of the loss of Terry Eddington. Few people live a life like Terry did. The words love, kindness, and generosity all describe him. I may not be family, but if I ever had a friend who I considered my brother, Terry Eddington was that friend.

RON SHORT

Ron Short contrasts physically with me, and in some ways we are also different in personalities and habits. Ron is huge. He towers over me. He isn't only strong physically, but is strong in other ways I find remarkable.

Ron Short is a larger than life friend who jumps to help me with any and all requests.

We became friends when I moved to Cranbrook to pastor the church he was attending with his wife Bonnie. I learned quickly that Ron has no off-switch. He is the quintessential energizer bunny. He gets up early in the morning, which contrasts with my slow entrance into each day. Ron also turns in very early and I tend to stay up later, but these are minor compared to the strength of heart I observe in my dear friend.

Prior to meeting Ron and Bonnie, I learned of their many tears. Ron struggled with addiction before meeting Jesus. This caused much trouble, but God drew Ron into an amazing relationship that resulted in him founding Wings as Eagles Recovery Centre. Wings as Eagles has helped hundreds of men break free from the destruction of alcohol and drug addiction. I had the joy of teaching there for many years.

In time, Ron was invited to become the pastor of The Dwelling Place. Ron also served as the head of the ministerial in Cranbrook, British Columbia. As I said, his energy is so different from mine. He just works and works and works.

Additionally, Ron saw his beloved wife Bonnie suffer with brain cancer. Surgery saved her life but also affected her in numerous ways. She became totally dependent on Ron. Can you imagine just how much weight Ron carried in his life? My respect for this man could not be greater. Bonnie sadly passed away in 2017. She was blessed with a husband of Ron's caliber.

With all the responsibilities and weight Ron carried, he made the time to be a true friend to me. I could sit over a coffee and share my struggles. This man, who had more than his own share of trouble, listened, prayed, and cared for me. Oh that we would all love others like Ron Short does. What a wonderful world we would live in if we could be so selfless.

True friendship not only gives, it gives when it's difficult to give. While Ron was attending the church where I pastored, I knew he was my armorbearer. He stepped in numerous times to protect and support me. I can't help but believe that God honored his selflessness when he became the pastor of The Dwelling Place. I was so disappointed to lose him to another church, but we have remained close while serving in other churches.

After some time, God blessed Ron with a wife and friend, Darlene, who would be his help and encouragement. I could not be more thrilled.

LILLIE BANKS

Lillie is the only single woman I mention here. I have women friends, but for modesty's sake they are connected to us through Carole. Lillie is a wonderful friend who I cherish.

Prior to Carole and me moving from Kansas City, we had to have a photo taken with this beautiful lady.

We met Lillie in 1992 when we moved to Kansas City. She sang in the church choir and quickly became a soloist and leader. Her strong mind and determination assisted her as an excellent single mother and a great example of godliness to many.

We moved from Kansas City in 2003, but we didn't move from Lillie's heart. Over the many years, this wonderful woman has not forgotten our birthdays, anniversary, or other important events in our lives. One thing I've learned about friendship is that a friend cares about what's important to you. Lillie is a perfect example of this. It's hard to imagine someone caring more than this little lady.

When we've had occasion to visit Kansas City, she has arranged a supper meeting with friends at a favorite restaurant. She has gone way beyond what one could expect a friend to do. She is an amazing person with such godly character that she has been asked to teach at the church. Her lessons undoubtedly reveal the greatness and love of Christ.

DR. HENRY SCHELLENBERG

*Henry Schellenberg is gifted man whom I consider to be
one of the finest men I've ever met.*

Some friends of mine have been professors whom Carole and I have had the honor to study with, including Jack Hunka, Chuck Nichols, Ed Neufeld, and Gus Konkel. Sadly, some have passed away. One man who we both loved and miss is Henry Schellenberg.

We first met Henry when we attended Winnipeg Bible College in the mid 1980s. Henry was teaching in the music department and we were pleased to be his students. He was a gentle, kindly, elegant man who could smile and giggle, but I can truthfully say that I never really heard him laugh. You know the kind of person... someone who doesn't belly laugh but still smiles. Carole's parents were like that, too.

Henry was a master conductor and a wonderful baritone singer. He earned his doctorate at Southern Methodist University. His style was precise, especially as he conducted the school choir in classics like The Messiah. I believe we also sang works by Haydn, such as The Creation and possibly The Seasons. Henry was a pleasure to study with and he made music fascinating through his relaxed style.

Carole and I were very blessed to be invited to have dinner with Henry and his wife Jocelyn at their home. This meant so much us at the time, but it meant even more a few short years later when Henry suffered an early death at the hands of cancer. He went to the hospital to visit someone who was a patient and collapsed. He lived longer, which was a blessing, but he succumbed to the illness to the sorrow of many, including his beautiful wife.

It has been suggested that in an average seventy-year lifetime, a person will know more than 1,800 people. Some friends will pass away, and other friends we'll lose track of as we move. For us, catching up with old friends through social media has been extra special. There have been times when we've connected with former friends only to find that the friendship never ended, even though decades had passed.

DARREN AND RACHELLE RONALD

I had the honor of officiating Darren and Rachelle's wedding.

There is a couple that stands out in my mind as the most unique, loving people you could ever meet. While I was pastoring in Cranbrook, a couple asked me to marry them. This has always been an honor and joy, but I must say that I've done more premarital counselling than officiating weddings. On this occasion, I was blessed to officiate the wedding of Darren and Rachelle.

Interestingly, the wedding day was my birthday, July 16. It was to be held outside in another city. Incidentally, most weddings I've performed in Canada have been held outside. In other nations, they were inside. Try and figure that one out!

We arrived and were told that a hotel room had been reserved for us. When we opened the door to our room, it looked like we were walking into a birthday party. Decorations and gifts had been lovingly left in the room.

The wedding reception turned out to be even more gripping. This selfless couple had made it into a birthday party with cake, gifts, and the singing of the birthday song. It was so embarrassing. This was their wedding, but they loved me so much that they made their wedding more about me. How do you explain that kind of love? Even now it brings a tear of such gratefulness to my eyes. Darren and Rachelle are my friends.

DR. GEORGE W. WESTLAKE JR.

George Westlake is not only my pastor, he is my friend.

It would be a mistake not to mention my pastor and friend, Dr. George Westlake. In the winter of 1991, he invited me to move from Saskatoon to Kansas City to become the music pastor at the church where he was senior pastor. Sheffield Family Life Center was a church of numerous ethnicities. Well more than a thousand people met every Sunday morning. When we left eleven years later, there were more than five thousand attending.

Pastor Westlake was a tremendous preacher, teacher, and pastor. People loved him for his transparency and amazing command of scripture, of which he could quote vast passages. He loved people of all ethnicities and it could be seen in the make-up of the church.

Apart from his skills, he has been a close friend. One sad day, I wept because he texted me minutes after his beloved wife Jean passed away. What kind of friend is that? He loved her deeply. They had been married for more than fifty years. In addition to giving me such an honor, he was always my first reference on my resume. He pastored Sheffield for more than thirty-five years.

Like a father, he had to discipline me when I wondered off, but he always loved Carole and me. He appreciated what we could bring to the church, but he never treated us as a commodity to be used. He treated us as friends.

My usual seat at Sheffield Family Life Center

There were three Sunday services at Sheffield. Pastor Westlake preached for all three while I played the piano, so we had many times to just talk between services. I'll never forget him telling me that one of the songs we had sung in the first service was too slow. I gently said, "Pastor, I wrote that song." He adjusted himself and I giggled.

I love George Westlake not just because I still regard him as my pastor, but also because I consider him to be my friend.

HERB KRUSCH

Herb and I were students together at Northwest Bible College. In 1983, we saw Herb and Christine at the Edmonton International Airport. We were flying to Ottawa to join the staff at Woodvale Pentecostal Church. Herb and Christine were on their way to Africa where they would serve faithfully as missionaries for many years.

In 2009, we reconnected after many years only to find out that Herb was suffering from ALS. His physical condition was quickly becoming life-threatening. Herb couldn't speak after a while, so he typed the following message to me:

John, I now use mostly a feeding tube and actually enjoy it. I have this 18-inch-long tube hanging from the top of my stomach. I can eat mushy food. I cannot use my tongue. I cannot suck on a straw, or blow very hard. I can't really spit. I choke very easily on food and have to be very careful. I get tired very easily, and I am weak.

I can only walk about 100 feet and have to rest. Most times my muscles hurt. I cannot do up buttons or tie a shoe lace. I cannot use scissors as my thumbs are weak. Most times it is hard to hold my head up, as my neck gets very sore. I often have shortness of breath. I use a breathing machine at night and have a face mask like a pilot that I wear at night. My breathing machine at night is a big relief. I look forward to it.

I cannot speak. I have to use a portable speaking machine now, but I prefer to bring my laptop as it is faster to type and have people just read it. Amazingly, I can still drive my Avalanche truck. I go out very seldom though. Chris and the kids and friends are a big support. My tube food and all supplies are supplied by the government as is all equipment, such as the breathing machine. The health care here is amazing and it is all free.

I have a strong faith in Jesus Christ. So, I am not afraid. As to my illness; I have never asked God "why?" I am totally at peace with his will. The Bible says, "To live is Christ, to die is gain." That means no matter what… I am at peace. The Bible also says, "O death where is your sting?" Because of my faith in Christ… I don't have to worry about what is going to happen when I die. There is absolutely no fear or doubt of my destiny. I have in no way ever had fear or anything come upon me. God is good! I have the privilege to have the time to prepare and say my goodbyes. If God chooses to heal me, well that would be great too, but as there is no cure, it would have to be of God. I leave that in his loving hands.

No matter what happens, His way is perfect and like the Bible says in Phil 4:6,7, "Be careful for nothing; but in every thing by prayer and supplication with thanksgiving let your requests be made known unto God. And the peace of God, which passeth all understanding, shall keep your hearts and minds through Christ Jesus."

Am I mad at God? Why should I even be mad at him? Look how much He has given me purpose and the means to fulfill his will. I have travelled the world, sharing his love and message. I have met so many amazing people and made so… many friends. He has given me Chris, and three healthy children, and one wonderful granddaughter. Our needs have always been met. God has provided hard times for me to grow. He has proven his love to me over and over again.

God has also given me time to prepare for death. "Death"… ha… like it is something bad. Better yet… God has given me time for a new phase of my life; a commencement… a new beginning! It is a graduation, a celebration of the purpose of the resurrection. The passing from this earth to Heaven; it is our destiny, it is our hope! See you there!

OTHER FRIENDS

It's always difficult to name names, since someone may be inadvertently missed. The list of people mentioned in this chapter is in no way exhaustive. I could tell the stories of my dear friends Richard Piech, Ken Russell, Darrell and Laura Alley, Jim and Colleen Guskjolen, Robert and Pam White, Jason Ramsay, Earl and Anita Downing, Rich and Dana Avila, Steve and Shauna Moon, Philip Brown, David Silver, Kerry and Shawndelle Pocha, Marvin Wojda, Dennis Carnahan, Bill and Deborah Gooding, Larry and Deborah Sims, Lyle and Irene Horrill, Willie and Vickie Murillo, Ian Bennett, Fel and Dianna Bagunu, Rocky and Dana Candillo, Doug Rooney, Diane and Danny Burrows, Chua Hock Lin and Dora Chua, Tom and Kathy Mitchell, David and Christine Morton, CK and Jaclyn Tan, Dave and Barb Devries, Jimmy Hoskins, and many others… but that would be another book.

Make no mistake. I have also lost friends. I am far from perfect and do make errors. I have shed tears at the thought of my actions several years ago that caused two friends to turn their backs on me and walk away. I cannot blame them. I caused them pain. I was careless with my words.

Here's a little secret I shouldn't share: if you want to hurt me, words won't do it as much as rejecting me as a friend.

There is a person I still consider a friend who will not speak to me. I have searched my actions repeatedly to find something I did, but she will not even hear an apology—even though I wouldn't know what I was apologizing for. This has caused me many tears, since she and I shared lots of laughs in the past.

The lesson in all of this, at least for me, is that friendship must be nurtured and protected. Careless words have severed relationships I thought would last for life. It's not the blatant unkind words that damage the most; it's the words that are spoken in ignorance that expose a lack of appreciation for a friend. I am guilty but purpose to be wise with relationships.

People will walk in and out of our lives, but our responsibility is to act in sensitivity to others. We may not always know what will hurt another, but we must go to great lengths to guard against careless words.

I value friendship more than gold. Friends see you through the tears and laugh with you. Many of the people I've written about here have laughed with me and sought me out to weep with me. Those are the kinds of people you want to seek out.

Solomon wrote, *"A friend is always loyal, and a brother is born to help in time of need"* (Proverbs 17:17, NLT). I can witness to the truth of this statement. My friends have become like family.

That's why it's difficult to name only a few, and it's likely some people will be forgotten.

The top of Eger Hill, overlooking the Purcell Mountains. Neil, Kirk, myself, Carole, Kerry, Lori and Kayla. Shawndelle took the picture.

Our many friends in Singapore gathering to pray with us and say goodbye.

The band I played with at New Life Church in Oak Grove, Missouri, including Barrie and Perry.

Our friends in Singapore, Pastor Joseph, Christine, and family, Lavanga and family.

There are three men who have had an impact on me by their unmistakable character: Laury Berteig, David Mainse, and Tommy Barnett. All three had the ability to talk to you like you were the only person in the world. Their attention was fixed on you when you were in conversation with them.

Laury was my music pastor, and he became a mentor and good friend. Sadly, I only briefly met David and Tommy, and I wish I could have known them as friends. All three were exceptional men of God. As models of Christian leadership, there could not be better.

Other friends who have since passed away include Mike McIntyre, Hugh McKee, and Calvin Hunt.

Jesus lost friends, too. One of the most touching scriptures is John 11:35, *"Jesus wept."* He loved his friends, and friendship was important to him. He was accused of being a friend of sinners (Matthew 11:19), and the truth is that he was. Being a friend of sinners wasn't a support of sinfulness, though. Jesus made it clear who he had come to call: *"It is not those who are healthy who need a physician, but those who are sick; I did not come to call the righteous, but sinners"* (Mark 2:17). The truth is that we were all sinners, because Jesus came for all of us. This is good news for everyone.

Occasionally, I have been warned about a person by those who that felt they were doing me a favor by speaking of that person's faults. Instead of avoiding him, however, I have decided to make those people my friends by being kind to them. The key for me is to look beyond a person's faults. For me, those weaknesses aren't important. What's important is that I treat others with kindness regardless of how they act. Could this be the way of Jesus? None of us were pure and sinless.

It's easy to give up on people and to even spread unkind words about them, but if we have grateful hearts for the love of God, we should win people over and not give up on them.

Let me encourage you to give to others. Give what, you ask? Give yourself to others as a friend. People desperately need your friendship. Even those who don't deserve it. Instead of avoiding them, we might want to intentionally seek out the marginalized, the dirty, and the ugly (so to speak) and seek to bring them healing and love. Who knows? They might even improve in areas where some believe they are deficient.

Suffice it to say, I greatly value friends and friendship.

Chapter Eight
CHURCH MINISTRY

In this chapter, I will highlight a few of the church ministries we have been privileged to be a part of. The great majority of my ministry years were spent as a music and worship pastor, but in some locations I also served in pastoral care, youth, and visitation ministries. Sometimes our stay was short for various reasons, so this chapter will be limited to those where we spent most years, including Edmonton, Saskatoon, Kansas City, Singapore, and Cranbrook.

I heard the call of God to serve in church ministry while I was still in high school. After taking three years of Bible college, a professor gave me the phone number of a pastor who was looking for a music pastor. I called Rev. Lyle Horrill and met with him. He became a good friend who Carole and I greatly admired and loved. He did our premarital counselling and married us.

The Clareview Pentecostal Church was growing, but along with Pastor Horrill there was a full-time youth pastor (Bob Bidwell) and the church didn't have the budget for a music pastor, even though they were hoping to find one. I met with the board and told them that while living at home, I only needed a small salary to cover my car payment, insurance, and gas. They told me that it was a reasonable request, but they didn't have the budget. A couple of weeks later, they called me to say that they still didn't have the budget but were going to hire me in faith that God was going to provide. Over three years, my salary tripled.

On Tuesday mornings, Pastor Horrill, Bob, and myself met at 7:00 a.m. for prayer and then went out for breakfast. We had a corner booth at the local Big Boys restaurant. Most weeks we would go to pay our bills only to have Pastor Horrill insist on paying. This happened frequently, so one week when I forgot to bring my wallet I thought I was safe. As I remember, Bob also wasn't ready to pay for his breakfast. Worry? Why? Pastor Horrill was like our dad, taking care of things. Only on this Tuesday, the pastor didn't have the funds to cover us. I don't recall what happened, but it was certain that we were all ready to pay for our breakfast from then on.

In front of the church, we had a sign up on a fifteen-foot post, and we changed the message on it every week. Taking a ladder and climbing to the top, one of us would rearrange the letters to announce the coming sermon or event.

One very cold week, it was my turn to do the job. It was freezing, so I took the ladder out and then went back inside to warm up. I went out, took down the letters, and again went inside to warm up. Finally, I went out and put the new message up.

Little did I know that the wind and cold were so extreme that I burned my face that day. It was very painful. Because I was suffering so much, the pastor's wife gave me some cream, which I applied liberally to my entire face. What I didn't know was that I was allergic to the cream. When I woke up the next day, my face had swollen so much that I could barely see. It didn't take long for the swelling to go down, and then the skin began to scale. I looked like a monster.

When Carole opened the door to her house that day—at the time, we were newly engaged—she was shocked to see how my face had been disfigured. It took a while for my skin to recover, but I still went to church. From the platform, Carole said, people wouldn't notice the skin peeling.

During my years at Clareview Church in Edmonton, I met Carole, married her, and administered an exciting music ministry that included seven choirs. We travelled with the youth choir and presented adult, youth, and children musicals. The young adult choir was named Master's Choice and the children's choir was Shepherd's Flock. Ministry in this church was exciting, very busy, and rewarding.

My next significant ministry assignment was serving as music pastor at Elim Tabernacle in Saskatoon. Again, one of my former professors had told me that a pastor was looking for a music pastor, so he gave me a phone number. I called Pastor George Johnson, met with him, and he hired me. The church was larger than Clareview and had a larger staff, including four other pastors. My salary was slightly improved, but my office was a tiny triangular room.

A well-known evangelist, Sam Farina, called Elim the Pepto Bismol Church since the pews were bright pink. When anyone opened the doors to the sanctuary for the first time, their eyes would widen in surprise. It truly was unique.

I had the choir there sing Brooklyn Tabernacle Choir songs, and they sang quite well. We also started an orchestra and a school of music. Not long after arriving, I convinced my parents to move to Saskatoon. Dad took over the school of music and played the organ. It was wonderful to have them close. Pastor Johnson then left and his associate, a friend of mine from Bible college days named Marvin Wojda, became the pastor.

On Tuesday mornings, I met with a friend from Jamaica, Ian Bennett, who was a university student. We always spent an hour in prayer on Tuesday before going for breakfast, just like I'd done while at Clareview. My trust in God and admiration for Ian grew as we brought our concerns to our Lord and Savior. Ian also sang in the choir and has remained a friend over the years. We don't see each other except for Facebook posts, but I treasure Ian and those valuable times.

From Saskatoon, Carole and I were thrilled to be invited to serve in Kansas City with Dr. George Westlake. The auditorium at Sheffield Life Family Center was packed for all three services every Sunday. It was obvious that building a new auditorium would be necessary. Other churches also grew in the city as a result of salvation coming to many people at Sheffield and then moving on to other churches. The new sanctuary, across the street, created more room that filled up quickly.

During our eleven years at Sheffield Family Life Center, we saw amazing and supernatural works of God. We arrived in 1992 to a church of 1,400 attendees, and there were 5,000 people every Sunday when we left.

The music ministry consisted of wonderful soloists and a few musicians. Kansas City is in the heart of jazz country, and the church was ethnically inclusive. About a third of the church were black, a third were white, a third were Hispanic, and the remainder were Asian. At the first rehearsal of our choir, there were thirty singers, and when we concluded ministry there the choir had grown to more than one hundred twenty people.

Over the years, we recorded four albums and toured with the choir. Our amazing rehearsals included times of prayer and worship. In fact, at one rehearsal we created an arrangement to a song just by worshipping. I started playing "Thou Art Worthy," then Darryl put a beat to it and we began to play it more joyfully. It was so great that we later recorded our version of the song. It wasn't uncommon for a soloist to grab a microphone and lead a song that hadn't been planned. That's what Teddy Rogers did that day. As we were singing "Thou Art worthy," Teddy stepped up to the microphone without being invited and ad libbed. It was inspiring.

We once received an invitation from the management of Celine Dion, the Canadian recording artist, to sing with her for a concert in Kansas City. I declined when I was told the songs we would sing. If we could sing about Jesus, we would have gladly accepted this honor. We had other invitations that I never shared with folks, since they weren't concrete and would only feed speculation.

On a tour through Texas, the choir stopped at a Golden Corral restaurant. We had two tour buses and more than 80 people who made their way in to have lunch. We were unmistakable, since we were all wearing the same T-shirt advertising our new album. The manager asked who we were, and once he knew it was a choir he invited us to sing. Jeff Hill and I ran out to the bus and brought in our keyboards. We sang for our lunch.

Many years later, when some members of the choir met for a reunion at Golden Corral, we sang a cappella to the delight of others in the restaurant.

The choir sang with passion and joy. We were never apologetic of our expressiveness. One producer who heard the choir once commented privately to me that Sheffield's choir was raw, genuine, and unpretentious. While we did have numerous singers with powerful gifts, most were ordinary folk who just loved God and enjoyed singing his praises. Some of our singers were so strong that we called them "big mouth voices." Carole was one of these. Sometimes people were surprised by the strength of voice that came from such little bodies.

The choir eventually outgrew the choir loft and platform, and we had to extend the platform.

We became very close with many in the choir. We walked with them through some horrible events, including the murder of children. I recall going to the hospital to sit with one of the sopranos. Her sons had been attacked in the inner city. One son had been killed, and the other was shot and was barely hanging on to life. How do you care for folk in such a situation other than weep with them?

A tenor in the choir had his stepson killed by an off-duty police officer. I sat in the courtroom for weeks and witnessed the man being found guilty and sentenced to prison, but it didn't comfort the grieving parents.

Other members who we loved endured difficult physical illnesses. Some passed away, but our memories of this beautiful choir and the heavenly times we had with them will never fade from my mind.

In addition to the choir, we started the Jesus Jazz Band. Initially, the instrumentation was a piano, two bass clarinets, an accordion, a guitar, a banjo, a guitar, a bass, and an organ. Over time, and with some creative work, the band morphed into a big band with six saxophones, four trombones, and five trumpets. Along with the horns we had people playing piano, organ, keyboard, drums, bass, guitar, and three people playing percussion.

So much could be written about the music ministry at Sheffield. It could be its own book!

One story that needs to be told here took place the night of a rehearsal with the Jesus Jazz Band. We rehearsed on Tuesdays at 7:00 p.m., and as I was pulling into the parking lot one evening I noticed that my gas gauge showed I was below the empty line.

Have you ever been in a situation where you had no cash and nothing in the bank? That night, I had no way to get home. We lived thirty minutes from the church, so I thought maybe I could borrow some cash from a friend at rehearsal.

The problem is that I forgot about my plight until I got back into my car more than two hours later. By the time I turned on the security system and locked the doors, everyone who had been at rehearsal was gone. As I sat in the car, I prayed and asked the Lord to help me. That he did. I turned on the ignition and saw the gas gauge increase to a quarter of a tank.

At the end of rehearsals, we spent time in prayer together. One Tuesday evening, as we stood in a circle, a friend shared that she and her husband had been devastated by the news that they would not be able to have children. It was wonderful to witness the sensitivity and empathy pour out as we prayed. A few months later, they were informed that although it wasn't supposed to have happened, the wife was pregnant.

Some may choose to doubt that prayer and faith in God has any value, but I'm convinced that it does. These are only two examples of how God has rewarded faith and trust in him with miracles.

Jesus Jazz Band, like the choir, were a group of ordinary people who loved to worship God with music. Most players had learned to play their instruments in high school and hadn't taken private lessons, but they really applied themselves. Their passion was to express the joy of the Lord through instrumental music, although periodically we had a singer from the choir do scat.

The Jesus Jazz Band was invited to play in shopping malls and on television, which was both enjoyable and an honor. There were very few groups like JJB, so the music we played had to be available and well written. Over the years, we collected charts by Camp Kirkland, Tom Payne, and a few other gifted arrangers.

While serving at Sheffield, I was protected with a miracle by God as I was driving home one day. After leaving the office, I drove up Topping Avenue and stopped at a red light. The light turned green, and I intended to pull out into the intersection, but before I could, the Holy Spirit prompted me to stop. I asked, "Why, Lord? The guy behind me will honk his horn." Nevertheless, I took my foot off the accelerator. I was amazed when a car that I hadn't seen raced through the red light on my left. If I hadn't obeyed, a horrific accident would have taken place with me being the primary victim.

Amazingly, a similar incident took place a second time, only I didn't obey. When I pressed the gas pedal, nothing happened. The engine didn't move. It didn't even rev. God had stopped my car from moving even after I'd ignored his voice. Once again, a vehicle ran the light, but God spared my life. No one can ever convince me that miracles don't happen.

The building we met in was a gym which connected to the chapel and office building. Many funny incidents took place there. For instance, a man once put on a costume and accosted a guest speaker, who frankly was full of himself. Jaimie, a member of the church, had long hair and a beard, so dressing in a robe and acting as though he was Jesus seemed like the thing to do. He thought a guest speaker needed a dose of humility. When the speaker walked around a corner, he found Jaimie pointing a finger pointing in his face, correcting him of his arrogance and pride. This must have been embarrassing for Pastor Westlake, but we all had a good laugh.

A man once showed up with his dog and wanted to preach, so he took a chair and was setting himself up on the platform when Pastor Westlake informed him that he would not be preaching. The ushers gently but firmly took the man out and made sure the dog didn't leave a gift.

I'll never forget watching a lady dance at the front of the platform one Sunday. People usually danced with the exuberant music, but this lady truly overdid it. She was making a show of it and was a distraction. I watched as Pastor Westlake caught the eye of the assistant pastor's wife, Brenda Wesley. He just nodded to her and she unassumingly danced over to the lady and took her by the arm. Then she danced the lady into the prayer room. What a wonderful way to deal with a difficult situation.

The gym had theatrical lights that were focused on the platform. While Pastor Westlake was preaching one Sunday, the lights began to flicker. Ushers ran off to discover Jeremy—yes, my son—behind the platform turning the switches on and off. Jeremy was young and had sneaked out of Sunday school. Afterward, a door was constructed to cover the control panel. It was named the Jeremy Door. I was the one who was embarrassed this time.

There were times when I had the unpleasant task of disciplining female choir members behind the platform for wearing short skirts. We dressed well. The men wore suits and ties and the women wore dresses or skirts. Sometimes we had matching vests, shirts, and dresses. The problem we faced was that the platform in the gym was so high that if a woman wore a short skirt, it would be a distraction, especially for the many pre-believers in attendance. We set a standard, but there were a couple of times when I felt the wrath of a woman. Once it was a soloist who was scheduled to sing on a Sunday night. I had to put my foot down and she had to turn around and go home to change. This was the difficult part of being a responsible pastor.

We got to record with famous singers such as Alvin Slaughter, Vickie Yohe, John Starnes, and Karen Wheaton. We also worked with the Nashville String Machine and horn players from Music City. It was a thrill to hear songs we'd written in the kitchen of our home on CD. In fact, the title track of one of the albums, "Headed for Jesus," had been written by Carole in a grocery store.

Rarely do I hear singers who can match those who made Sheffield their home church. Sometimes when a talent show is on television and a singer performs, I remember the exceptional singers we were blessed to work with, including James, Nicole, Teddy, Tawnya, Marilyn, Bridget, Brenda, Art, Bill, Esther, and Mike. So many of them had voices to easily match those on television, but fame wasn't their motive. These weren't only amazing singers, they were godly people who sang in total worship of their creator. I'm not sure how all the talent came together at Sheffield when we were there. It had to be a God thing.

The musicians at Sheffield were equally exceptional, but it hadn't always been that way. There came a time when we had no piano player to lead the singing or choir, so I played for three services, two weekly rehearsals, and for the Wednesday evening service. It got to the point where even when I had pneumonia, bronchitis, and two ear infections, I had to go to church. Hearing the song leader, Pastor Fel, was difficult, so I didn't play by ear; I played by watching his lips and feeling the lower tones of the bass guitar.

Over time, we were blessed to have the Hill family begin attending. Jeff is an exceptional organist, piano player, and keyboardist. His brother Darryl was a steady drummer in two ways. He kept the beat constant, which is so important for a drummer, and he was also consistently available to play. In fact, Darryl played drums for years without a break. We became so familiar with each other that I didn't have to indicate where I was going with a song. He beautifully anticipated me.

Along with Jeff and Darryl, Stan, Mike, Jewell, Aaron, Raymond, Rahn, Dee, and my good friend Earl anchored the rhythm section for years. What a joy it was to work with these quality folks.

Over the eleven years that we were at Sheffield, we worked with numerous musicians, including Rosemary. We loved her beautiful spirit, but she went to Malawi. She was married there and now serves with her husband Moffat by pastoring Victory Christian Temple in Mzuzu.

While in Brooklyn for a pastors conference, I was surprised to see these old friends all the way from Malawi. When I sat in the auditorium of Brooklyn Tabernacle, I noticed the two heads in front of me. I tapped them on the shoulders and, sure enough, it was Moffat and Rosemary. Oh the joy we felt as we hugged and danced with delight.

Another highlight of our time in Kansas City was playing second keyboard for recording artist Carmen. His music is colorful and very descriptive. It's also difficult to play. The other musicians in his band were world-class, so I felt honored but inadequate. I attempted to prepare but found that I only contributed little, so I asked the sound engineers to keep me very low in the mix. They smiled and agreed.

I wish I could find a photo Carmen and I took together. As you know, I'm quite short, but what you may not know is that Carmen is very tall.

When I left the church, they didn't really miss me. That might be a hit to one's ego, but it was gratifying to know that the ministry wasn't about John and Carole Telman. It was a team. Pastor Westlake used to call us a family and play the Pointer Sisters song "We Are Family" while we greeted each other. He was right.

Our next stop in ministry was Singapore. A good friend, Irvin Rutherford, was asked by Pastor Rick Seaward of Victory Family Centre in Singapore if he knew someone who could serve as General Overseer of worship for the church.

"I know of one guy, but he's in Canada," Irvin said.

Pastor Rick replied, "No problem," and then flew me to Hawaii to interview in a hotel room. He then sent me on to Singapore to meet people and to decide if I was going to accept the invitation to serve at Victory Family Centre. This church is very different than any I had ever experienced.

VFC was planted by Pastor Rick in the 70s.[31] He determined that they would plant churches through missional efforts all over the world, and that's what they

---

[31] Sadly, Pastor Rick Seaward was killed in a traffic accident in Brazil on March 24, 2018. We grieved with thousands around the world at this news.

did from the beginning. They train the best people in the congregation and send them to many nations, resulting in over one thousand VFC-mothered churches around the world. There were ninety thousand documented decisions made for Jesus Christ due to their efforts. In Singapore, the church of six thousand met in six English-speaking congregations, six Mandarin-speaking congregations, and congregations in nine other languages.

Me leading worship in the central part of Singapore.

Twice a year, the church would meet in a stadium, with interpreters speaking through headphones. Every Sunday evening, the church met in two locations and simulcast the service so that one site could host the preacher and the other site could host the music team. Into this incredible situation, I was called to administer and guide a worship ministry that included twenty-nine drummers, more than thirty guitar players, and many bass players, piano players, and singers. Carole and I learned that Asians emphasize prayer. Tuesdays were prayer meeting night in all the church's locations, and it was dynamic.

Since Singapore is only miles from the equator, the temperature doesn't vary all that much. Many activities of the church were held outside. Baptisms were held in the South China Sea. Fellowship meals were outside. Funerals were held outside. Restaurants were al fresco. We even presented a Christmas musical outside. That night, I played piano.

On the final Tuesday evening before we moved back to Canada, I shared about having an eternal perspective. I told the congregation that heaven is so close, and I even jumped with the expectation that I could be raptured at any moment.

After sitting down, "Uncle" Ronnie Lim, who was a greeter, gave his testimony. Uncle Ronnie loved people. His smile was infectious, so he wasn't called Mr. Lim or Ronnie. He could only be called Uncle Ronnie. You felt loved when he was around.

Following my talk, Ronnie shared about how my words had reminded him of his family and friend who had accepted Jesus and passed away. He told us that he was looking forward to seeing these people again and believed that they had been freed from time and other impediments of this temporal life.

Uncle Ronnie then sat down behind me and died. Yes, you read that correctly; he died minutes after I shared about having an eternal perspective. Usually when a person has a heart attack, their face grimaces, but not Uncle Ronnie. He wore a look of peace and eternity that I will never forget.

Not only were we amazed by this unique church, we were also amazed by the food we ate in Singapore. Some have stated that Singapore perfects the foods of the world. Carole and I can testify to the wonderful tastes we experienced, including tissue prata, hot-pot, cendol, and many other culinary treats.

In addition to the amazing food and culture, we noticed that the churches in Singapore truly thrived. Victory Family Center wasn't the only church there that sent thousands of people into missions. There are numerous mega churches in this largely Buddhist nation. We were instructed to be cautious in evangelism while living in Singapore, but people were coming to Christ in large numbers.

Carole and I were privileged to also plant a church, Victory International Church (VIC). Since Singapore was a haven for expatriates from around the world, the pastor wanted us to reach out to different ethnicities. Chua Hock Lin, his wife Dora, Carole, and I began to meet and plan. We learned of some friends, Dr. Kathy and Mark Wallace, who had recently moved to Singapore where Kathy was going to teach music at the university. We met with them and they became a large part of the growth of Victory International Church. Over the years, the ministry has succeeded in reaching many expats with the gospel.

My doctoral dissertation argued for an ethnically inclusive church. As Pastor Westlake said, "It looks like the kingdom of God." This will be what heaven looks like—every tribe and tongue worshipping the creator.

This is a photo of the Victory Family Church staff fun day.

Organizationally, Victory Family Center followed the G12 method. This meant that every leader had twelve people they would mentor and train. I was, of course, part of the pastor's twelve, although he had many pastors who assisted him. In fact, there were sixty-nine pastors in total.

Me with my twelve disciples. These men each had their own twelve, and so on. It was a pleasure to pray and study scripture with these godly men.

This little mountain church is where I had the honor of serving.

The first church I served at as lead pastor was Abundant Life Church in Cranbrook. It was a very small church that had experienced several difficult problems, including the suicide of their pastor. I don't want to focus on the hurts, though, but rather the victories and work of God. Over time, we saw miracles of God's grace and mercy.

Every time the building was open, whether on Sunday or when I was in the office, we would hang a sign on a post outside. Many who drove or walked past would read that sign and come in for prayer. Numerous instances over the years proved that God knew what he was doing when he instructed us to use this sign.

Here's an example of the value of this sign. One day, a man came in for healing prayer. He then returned later to let me know that he had been healed and that he now believed in God and his power to help those who asked and believed. Another time, a lady who suffered with depression and fear saw the sign and came in for prayer. She felt a tangible change in her life after we prayed for her, and she returned a few times to tell me that she was doing much better. Her joy was so real that she gave a substantial financial gift to the church. Most of those who came in for prayer never ended up attending services or becoming members, but it was a way to serve the community. Most of all, we were being obedient to God.

Sadly, Abundant Life Church was vandalized thirteen times in eleven months. People spray-painted nasty words on our church sign, broke in, destroyed the safe, and stole what little money we had. The doors were damaged so much that you could see through cracks. We shed many tears as we appealed to the Lord for help.

Over time, we made repairs, but it was unnerving and challenging to know that we were in a spiritual war. Incidentally, some years before we moved to Cranbrook, the former pastor had gone to the church one Sunday to find the doors chained and locked with deadbolts. This church had been a target ever since the enemy knew that it was a place where people would be freed from chains, healed, and saved.

We did battle with evil. A report came to us one day that witches were cursing the church. Considering all the trouble the church had experienced, who among us didn't believe their attack was real? We weren't about to let this go unchallenged. Prayer was not an optional activity, it was necessary.

A famed psychic was scheduled to come to Cranbrook, so we went to prayer asking God to protect the city from that which is forbidden in scripture (Leviticus 20, Deuteronomy 18, 2 Corinthians 11, Acts16). Divination is a false hope that leads people to seek to replace God as their help. We prayed, and we prayed again, and we kept praying. God answered our prayers for the city and this psychic had to cancel her appearance. As I recall, not enough tickets were sold, which was one of our direct prayers.

There was a wheelchair-bound man who was brought to the church services one day. The person who helped him each week moved away, however, and no one in this little church could pick the man up, so it fell to me. For more than five years, every Sunday and Wednesday, I went to the nursing home where he lived and drove him to church. Some years before, he'd had a massive stroke and couldn't walk. He could only stand for long enough to fall into the passenger seat of my car.

One Wednesday evening after prayer meeting, I took him to the car. He stood as usual, but as I pulled the wheelchair away to put it in the trunk, his pants fell to the ground. He couldn't reach down, so I let go of the wheelchair and quickly picked his pants up before passersby saw what had happened. What I didn't realize was that the wheelchair went flying into the road and was rolling towards traffic. I turned and ran to stop it, but dropped his pants. He yelled, and I didn't know what to do. I helped him get his pants up and helped him get his belt tightened. Then I ran down Eleventh Avenue to retrieve the wheelchair, hoping it didn't hit a parked car.

After taking this gentleman home, I sat in my car and asked, "Why me, Lord?" That may sound funny, but at the time I was serious. Being a pastor sometimes means picking up some person's pants who cannot do it for himself.

I was once encouraged to take time to visit an elderly man in a nursing home. Howard had been a church member for years. He was a kindly man, more than ninety years old, who loved these visits. Every Friday afternoon I went to see him and share what I was going to preach on Sunday. As he was a shut-in, he really enjoyed hearing a bit of the sermon. Sometimes he was so inspired that he would burst out with a hymn as I read scripture. When I closed our time together in prayer, he would grab my hands and pray a blessing over me. It was precious.

Howard had been a pilot in the Canadian Air Force during World War II and told me that he had landed in Singapore many decades before I lived there. He regaled me with stories that meant much to him.

Little did I know that Howard was a millionaire who had named the little church in his will. With that gift, we would be able to pay off the mortgage and do some desperately needed renovations. This was wonderful, but the thing that sticks with me most is that the moment he passed away, he cried out to the nurses around him that he saw an angel in his room inviting him to come. As a pastor, this impressed on me the need to be faithful in all things, no matter how insignificant they may seem.

I could write about being visited by angels in my office or about the healing God has performed in people's lives who were once hurt, but the most wonderful experiences were when I witnessed the baptism of new believers. Pastors treasure the joy of spiritual birth.

To celebrate with joy, we quarterly called our Sunday service the Praise Party. We sang songs and gave testimonies of the goodness and love of God. I didn't preach, and we shared a meal together. Some of the stories shared included remarkable instances of God's healing touch or saving grace. The Praise Party was a service the congregation always looked forward to.

As a pastor, I have officiated many weddings and funerals. I felt drained at the end of a dark period where I had to officiate three funerals for four different people.

One Monday evening, I had received a call telling me that one of our members and her daughter had been killed in a car accident. Carole and I met the husband who was crushed, and he and I went to see the body of his beloved wife and his only daughter. The church was full of people wanting to say goodbye to these two lovely ladies.

I was also called on to officiate a funeral for a man who had committed suicide by driving his car head-on into a truck on a highway. Again, the hall was packed with people who had questions and lots of tears.

A second suicide was highly difficult because the man's teenaged son had found his body. At times like that, a pastor feels so emptied of the ability to help, but I purposed to remind these folks that Jesus knows about sorrow. Jesus wept at a friend's tomb and then told his disciples that the tears would be only temporary. I also committed to be available to the wife and her boys. This seemed so inadequate to me, but in situations like that there isn't much we can do. We have to totally rely on the strength and help of God.

Isn't that the point of ministry? Ministry, no matter if it's music, preaching, praying, or listening, is about pointing people to Jesus and his heart of love for all people. I may not be the greatest orator and I may not be a gifted counsellor, but what I can attempt to be good at is turning people to Jesus. In other words, I'm just an arrow pointing to the one who understands, cares, listens, feels our pain, heals, and restores our lives.

Earlier, I mentioned that Carole worked in the nursery when the congregation grew and families with children were added. The children became a wonderful part of the church. Sometimes they would join the adults for Sunday morning service, and when they did, two of the girls liked to take notes of my sermons. They showed attentiveness. One of the girls took notes by drawing pictures, but both gave me what they'd written down—and what a thrill it was to post them in my office!

We were told that Eleventh Avenue, the main road beside the church, was going to be repaved. It was in horrible condition, so we were very pleased about the news. The other roads around the church were paved, but Eleventh was in rough shape. The first day I saw workers, I found out who the foreman was and told him that we wanted to thank them for doing this work during the heat of the summer.

I also told him that we, as a church, wanted to host the construction crew for a lunch a couple of times while they were working the project. They happily agreed, so we set up a shade tent and tables for the fifteen men. We also left an ice chest full of water for them and told them that the church bathrooms would be available while the office was open. Before they finished the job, I gave them a copy of my second book, *Making the Connection: Discovering Who God Really Is.*

One memorable evening took place during a board meeting. The six of us were seated around a table discussing the church when we heard a horrible bang.

The whole building shook, sending us running for the doors. What could have happened? Apparently, one of the board members had driven her motor home to the meeting and its propane tank had exploded in the parking lot. The RV was on fire when we reached it. There had been no one in it, except a tiny dog. He survived but was singed and probably had hearing loss.

Most of our board meetings were uneventful. We were so glad that the fire department kept the church building from catching fire. The incident shook us, but we were glad that further damage didn't take place. We are grateful for God's protection and help.

Over the years in Cranbrook, I preached close to four hundred times. Carole was such a great assistance to me when she wasn't serving in the nursery. Since she is the Old Testament scholar in our home, I would check with her about the accuracy of Hebrew words and passages. I hadn't studied Hebrew in college or seminary. My trust in her wisdom and balance in exegeting a passage caused me to often look toward her as I preached. Most of the time I would get an affirming look, but there were times when I saw her head bowed, gently shaking it as she silently mouthed "No." It was at times like when I had to be fast on my feet, back track, and save what I was sharing.

Peter, Marjorie and Katara began attending because of our excellent children's ministry. Carole and I were so overjoyed to see God working in this beautiful family.

Although the church never became large under my ministry, it did grow, and it did witness the greatness and mercy of God. Its place of ministry and usefulness in the kingdom of God cannot be minimized. Carole and I were blessed and honored to serve there and to enjoy the works of God in redeeming people, healing bodies, and touching the community.

The next stop in our lives was Ottumwa, Iowa, where I currently serve as lead pastor of Hickory Grove Community Church.

As one walks through the entrance hall leading to the church offices, there's a room designated the Prayer Closet. This is a small room reserved for nothing but prayer. Isn't that what we all need? It's vital to have a place to stop, drop, and pray. The church's choice to dedicate a room for this purpose impacted our decision to accept the call.

Additionally, the church had an area cut out of the hickory grove surrounding the church, and they named it Inspiration Point, a place where people could sit and pray in the beauty of God's creation. It's common to hear stories of the appearance of angels there.

All the churches where Carole and I have had the honor to serve have been uniquely placed and built by the master builder Jesus Christ. He told his disciple Peter, *"I will build My church"* (Matthew 16:18). Some may have missed the message of this passage by focusing on Peter, but the point is that Jesus is the builder. No pastor, preacher, or personality builds the church. Lights, music, activities, and programs do not build the church. Jesus does. After all, it's his church, isn't it? We would do well to focus on Jesus and not the temporal things that have no value apart from the touch of the Lord.

Over many years, Carole and I have ministered in more than these few churches. Our ministry included almost a month in Colombia. Both Carole and I preached twice at a most remarkable church there with a congregation of more than two hundred thousand people. Yes, you read that correctly. Almost a quarter of a million people are members of Misión Carismática Internacional. We attended services held in a stadium and were at early morning prayer meetings with hundreds of people in a huge hall. When we spoke, we did so at one of the cell church meetings of only a few hundred, but the ministry was highly impactful.

It was also an honor and joy to be a guest speaker in Indonesia for a singles weekend.

We've guested in many churches around the world, but the one theme we hold to is turning people to the reality of who God is. God heals, saves, sustains, and does so much that we just take for granted. The church isn't meant for anything other than the glory of God. When God is reflected in the church, through its love, kindness, and goodness, people are given a glimpse of who God is.

Ministry is interesting, to say the least. Sometimes it's exciting and you feel like you could jump over a wall. One Sunday, I was preaching in a church where a friend was pastoring. After the service, I stood outside in the beautiful summer sunshine, talking to a woman. Suddenly, another woman walked up to us and said, "That sermon was stupid and you're stupid." With that, she turned and walked away. Sometimes you feel like you've just run into a wall. What most people don't know is that ministry means caring for people even if they tell you something that disturbs you.

In another church, I noticed two ladies in conflict. They tried to hide it, but I could sense that something was dividing them. I brought them together to my office to talk it over. This reminded me of what the apostle Paul wrote, *"I urge you Euodia and I urge Syntyche to live in harmony in the Lord"* (Philippians 4:2). My hope was that we could talk it out, pray together, and be friends. Boy was I wrong. It was like two ferocious animals tearing at each other. Sadly, to my knowledge, their problem was never resolved.

I don't believe we need to relate directly with everyone. My nose is glad that my armpit is a distance away from it, but we can be civil, kind, and patient.

Let me remind you that it's the kindness of God that leads to us repentance, not his anger. The apostle Paul wrote, *"Or do you think lightly of the riches of His kindness and tolerance and patience, not knowing that the kindness of God leads you to repentance?"* (Romans 2:4) Paul didn't repent of having people persecuted and killed because God was mad, but rather because God was kind to him. Paul could have been destroyed for his actions against God's church, but instead he received kindness.

When the church keeps its focus on Jesus and the beauty of who he is, people are led to repent of their sin. Through that, he builds his church. If Carole and I have learned anything in our travels, it's this. We preach Christ. If we preached doing right or following the rules, there would be no power to change our hearts. But preaching Jesus grants us his help, his grace, to make us new.

Throughout our experiences, we've had laughs and tears in church ministry. We've wept in prayer for people who suffered and laughed in joy with others. We hold close to our hearts deep gratitude for the acceptance of our congregations and staff.

Epilogue
HOPES AND PRAYERS

The final sentence in my father's book was "The story continues."[32] Long after I'm gone, the story will continue, because the story is of the creator who lovingly cares for his creation. Someone once said that history is *his story*. Surely you must have noticed a thread winding through each chapter in this book, revealing the interaction of God in the lives of ordinary people. He was involved from the beginning and he will be involved until the end.

I needed a haircut one day, so I walked into a shop and had a conversation with a stylist while she worked on my hair. I made a friend with Yetty, a woman from Nigeria. As we were talking, I found out that she was a worship leader in a church in Saskatoon. When I told her that I had been a worship pastor for twenty years, she paused, and I wondered what she was thinking. She needed encouragement and God had appointed me give it. She believed that God had brought me to her.

After she did a great job on my hair, she wanted to take a picture with me. She was also amazed that Carole taught at Horizon College and Seminary, since she was going to be a freshman there the next year and was going to be studying with Carole. Wow! I gave her one of my books and gained a new friend to include in our devotional prayer time.

There is a belief called deism which claims that God did create the world but then he left it to its own devices. By this view, whatever happens is our doing and we must live with it. I unequivocally state here that this is patently false and has not been my experience. God is involved in our lives, whether we notice it or not.

---

[32] Telman, *A Laugh and a Tear*, 315.

The test is to open our eyes and observe just what God is doing. Being a customer of Yetty that day was no accident. It was God directing my steps without me even knowing why.

God does save. He heals, provides, and is very much a part of our lives. Those who counter that my life has been safe and free from the troubles others have need to read this book again. I haven't been born with the proverbial silver spoon in my mouth. I have experienced want, sickness, pain, and the loss of family, but God has heard my cry and answered. Is John Telman special? I suppose so. But then again, you are too—and so it everyone else. God doesn't play favorites when it comes to his love, care, and kindness.

Scripture is replete with inclusive language. *"For God so loved the world…"* *(John 3:16) and "He himself is the sacrifice that atones for our sins—and not only our sins but the sins of all the world"* (1 John 2:2, NLT) remind us that everyone is a candidate for God's love and care.

My friend, please realize that God does truly love you. The fact that you've had troubles doesn't mean he doesn't care. My prayer for you is that you will praise God for who he is regardless of what happens to you. He has permitted things to happen in our lives so that we will turn to him. Our true issue has always been that we turned away from him and went our own way. As Isaiah 43:6 says, *"All of us, like sheep, have strayed away. We have left God's paths to follow our own. Yet the Lord laid on [Jesus] the sins of us all"* (Isaiah 53:6, NLT). God has given us the freedom to choose him and his plan for our lives or to defiantly follow the pattern set by Adam and Eve. Instead of embracing the wisdom and guidance of the creator, they believed and acted like they knew better.

Tov is a Hebrew word meaning "useful or functional." In English, it's translated as *good*. *Mazel tov* is a Jewish blessing meaning "may goodness drip from above." God the creator is good, and he alone knows what is *Tov* (useful, functional, or good). We, on the other hand, are created beings. Apart from what God has declared good, we don't know what is good. God's plan was to have man live and enjoy what he himself said was good. God said that what he created was *tov*, and man was the recipient of this perfection.

Imagine telling God that his plans and purposes aren't good enough—but that's what we all have done. Instead of believing God and trusting him, all of us have sinned. We have told the creator that we know better. God created us and has purposes and plans that are useful. They are functional. They are *tov*. They're good!

Proverbs 19:21 reminds us, *"You can make many plans, but the Lord's purpose will prevail"* (NLT). Mankind can say that up is down, that wood is a drink, and that sin is good, but God is the creator and his plans and purposes will prevail. We should grieve over a man who thinks he's a woman. We should pray for those who think it's good to abuse alcohol and drugs.

Some horrible day, each and every one of us will bow before the one whose purposes and plans will prevail. At that moment, people will cry out, "What have I done to myself?" We have compassion for those who live by what they say is good. Some day they will realize that what they thought was good was not good. They were lied to by the Father of lies and they believed him, just like Eve did.

God's purposes and plans are *tov*. They're good! They're useful and functional. His purposes and plans are for life—and by the way, he is the life. He alone pronounces life. Life does not happen without him.

In the United States,

- Every eight seconds, a child drops out of school.
- Every twenty-six seconds, a child runs away from home.
- Every forty-seven seconds, a child is either abused or neglected.
- Every seven minutes, a child is arrested for a drug offense.
- Every thirty-six minutes, a child is either hurt or killed by a gun.[33]

This is not good. God is good and declares that his purposes and plans are good. You or I might not like it, but the absolute truth is that God is the one and only who decides what is good.

I won't forget that as a teenager I grappled with this question: why are some things wrong? Is God a killjoy? Is there something God doesn't want me to know that would be fun? Why are some things sinful? Some may also ask, why did God put tree in the garden that Adam was not to take fruit from?

God is the total authority. He instructs what is good and what isn't. Does the liar ask God if he should lie? Does the murderer ask God if he should kill? Instead of questioning God, we are wise to choose to obey God. He knows what is life and what is good. The enemy is the enemy. He has no interest in life.

Placing the tree of the knowledge of good and evil within reach was not a temptation, but Satan used it to bring doubt. In other words, he caused Adam and Eve to ask, "Does God really know what is good? Maybe you just misunderstand God." Mankind has largely listened to the lies of Satan and has taken fruit and eaten it.

God instructs us not to keep good from us. He knows what is good! The first five books of the Bible—Genesis, Exodus, Leviticus, Numbers and

---

[33] Peter W. Cookson Jr., *School Choice: The Struggle for the Soul of American Education, Revised Edition* (New Haven, CT: Yale University Press, 1995), 3.

Deuteronomy—are the Torah, which in Hebrew literally means "teaching." Even though mankind has arrogantly decided what is good, God has taught us was is good.

Imagine a child telling an adult that they believe one plus one equals eighteen, or that drinking poison is good. The adult would say, "Wait a minute! Let me teach you what is fact and what is good." God doesn't keep us from good, since he alone knows what is good. In fact, Israel sang this song:

> *Good and upright is the Lord; therefore He instructs sinners in the way. He leads the humble in justice, and He teaches the humble His way. All the paths of the Lord are lovingkindness and truth To those who keep His covenant and His testimonies.* (Psalm 25:8–10)

When God created the world, he made a garden that some think was hundreds of acres with thousands of trees that had fruit of all kinds. The choices were many and there was only one tree to avoid. God's instructions are not restrictive. They guard us as we humbly understand that our loving creator has given us boundaries so that we might know and experience his loving care.

1 John 5:3 says, *"Loving God means keeping his commandments, and his commandments are not burdensome"* (NLT). Remember to think of God's commandments as instructions for good and not heavy chains of dos and don'ts. God's instructions are prescriptions for life, health, and joy.

God not only instructs us, he also proclaims the appropriate consequences for ignoring his instructions. When we rebel against God, we hurt ourselves. We were created by God, so when we rebel there are terrible consequences now and forever. The consequences of sin and rebelling against a loving God doesn't always show up right away. They're like a sickness that you don't know about until years of smoking results in emphysema, or years of alcohol abuse results in liver cancer.

When anyone sins, it's the same as telling God that what he says isn't good enough. People can deny that God is good, and they can even complain about the consequences of their actions, but that doesn't change the fact that God the creator knows what is good and he alone set those consequences.

As God created, he said that things were good. The only thing that wasn't good was that man was alone, so he created a woman. He didn't create another man when something wasn't good. God declared what was good. Some listen to the lie of Satan and decide what is good, but God alone is the judge of what is good.

Notice that what was not good was the absence of something good. Darkness is the absence of light. Death is the absence of the author of life. God only created good things. Begin to see the greatness of the creator. He is worthy to be praised, but he is also worthy to be followed and obeyed.

The psalmist wrote, "O taste and see that the Lord is good; how blessed is the man who takes refuge in Him!" (Psalm 34:8) If you're a Christian and you fear or worry, are you saying that what God says isn't good enough?

A rich, young ruler once ran up to Jesus and asked, *"Good Teacher, what shall I do to inherit eternal life?"* (Mark 10:17) No rabbi was ever called "good." It was understood that only God is good. Jesus challenged this man with who he is. Jesus knew exactly what the man meant when he said used the phrase "Good Teacher." It's as if Jesus said, "Do you really know what you are saying when you call me good?" He is good. His name is Yeshua, which literally means "God is salvation." His name is not about punishment; it's about salvation.

God isn't willing that anyone should perish, and yet this rich young ruler wanted to know what he could do to have eternal life. He didn't want Jesus to be his Savior; he wanted Jesus to show him a way to be his own Savior. But Jesus is God, and this man needed to know that only God is good. Believe it or not, a pastor recently contacted me and, if you can believe it, he asked me if Jesus was God. I answered with one word: "Is."

Yeshua *is* good. Only God is good, and only he knows what is good. Everything in this world rests on the truth that he alone is good. That should impress on our hearts and minds just how important it is to pray and ask for his guidance.

When you eat, and you taste something that you really like, you may say, "This is really *tov*. This is really good!" Respectfully, how do you know? Only God knows what is good, and he has made it clear what is good. If you aren't sure what a good decision is, pray! Not only does God know what is good, he is good.

Some deceived people will cry in Arabic "God is great" and then attempt to kill people, but hear me: God is good. No one can deny the presence of evil in this world when they watch the news. Sadly, most do not believe that God is good. They believe the lie that each one knows better than the creator. Struggles and conflict takes place because man thinks he knows better than God.

Maybe you're struggling with something that has happened and the temptation to mistrust God has been whispered in your ear. Resist the enemy of your soul and place your trust in God.

The prophet Nahum said, *"The Lord is good, a stronghold in the day of trouble, and He knows those who take refuge in Him"* (Nahum 1:7) Moses was a man who knew God. One day he asked God to let him say his glory. Instead of his glory, God showed him his goodness (Exodus 33:19).

You have experienced, and you will experience, trouble and pain. Additionally, you will experience things you like, but God will be good to you all along your journey. I have experienced such things. The physical, emotional, and mental pain in my life has been so acute that I felt like I couldn't move.

On one dark day in our home, Carole and I sat in our living room, paralyzed with pain. We couldn't move. A friend called and offered to bring food over, but we both said, "Please don't. We wouldn't be able to chew." Suffice it to say that what we experienced was horrible, yet God was still good, and he healed our hurt hearts.

Life will also be wonderful. You will feel like you're on top of a mountain. It's equally important to recognize that God is good at this point. Should we forget the goodness of God when we're experiencing what we like? If we do, we will become ungrateful, self-dependent, and possibly arrogant.

My hope is that you will see and experience God for who he is and understand that Jesus Christ is your Lord and Savior, if you will only humble yourself in faith. Scripture tells us, *"For by grace you have been saved through faith; and that not of yourselves, it is the gift of God; not as a result of works, so that no one may boast"* (Ephesians 2:8–9). In Greek, the word that's translated here as grace is *charis. Charis* means more than favor. In this verse, it literally means that you are saved by the help and influence of God.

Our biggest problem is that we've all sinned and have a broken relationship with the creator, but we're also incapable of helping ourselves. This is much like a person dying from a terrible disease. He or she is dependent on someone else in many ways, including on a surgeon. We all need the *charis* of God to repair what we have broken—our very lives.

The good news is that God is more willing to give, heal us, and give everlasting life than we are to receive it. If we will only come to the place of crying out to God in repentance and surrendering to his ability to make us new, he will certainly do what we cannot.

Carole often reminds me to wear my glasses when driving. Without them, I find it hard to see the white line. When the sun goes down, the problem becomes more acute.

My brother-in-law Mark, who is a missionary in the Philippines, once told me that the white line is analogous to the Holy Spirit.

"The Holy Spirit is forever before us, guiding us, as we keep our focus directly toward him," Mark said. "The lights of approaching vehicles can be understood as representing life's challenges and problems. When one's focus is fixed on the problem or challenge, the risk is far greater."

With the white line in sight, you and I can steer the car accurately. The white line is a vital guide to all who drive vehicles. Have you ever noticed the confusion and danger that takes place when ice and snow blurs the white line? Chaos can easily result when this guide is blinded from one's view. In addition to the difficulty the elements can bring, so can the lights of an oncoming car. Focusing on those lights will draw a driver directly into its path. It's dangerous to watch the lights as opposed to the white line. Remember, the white line is the guide. The lights are indicators of an approaching object.

In John 14:1, Jesus implored the disciples, *"Do not let your heart be troubled."* He went on to make assurances of God about the Holy Spirit's involvement in our lives: *"He will teach you all things, and bring to your remembrance all that I said to you"* (John 14:26). God, like the white line, is always there. The problems you and I face, like those bright headlights, will pass from our experience.

Just as we often do, Peter asked questions that have little to do with building trust in God. Those questions drip from our lips with nervous impetuousness. What do I do now? Why did that happen to me? How am I going to get through this?

Jesus, after prophesying that Peter would be mesmerized by fear and deny him, gently taught us all about calmly redirecting our inner eyes once again on God: *"Truly, truly, I say to you, a rooster will not crow until you deny Me three times"* (John 13:38).

As John 14:1 says, *"Do not let your heart be troubled; believe in God, believe also in Me"* (John 14:1) The great teacher showed us that the issues we believe to be insurmountable are but passing. They're only dangerous if we look to them instead of God. Our destination can only be reached when we follow the white line of God's merciful guidance and refuse to be distracted or destroyed by what comes at us along the road of life.

I pray that throughout this book you have noticed that God loves and cares for us all. John Telman is no more special than you are. You are the object of his deep and undying love. Oh, how he wants to be a part of your life. He wants to be your everything.

Will you now pray and ask him to be your Lord and Savior? I am confident that he will change you for the better. You will experience another laugh and another tear, but you won't be alone. You will have the greatest friend to call on. Additionally, you will become a part of God's family, who will laugh and cry with you.

Over the years, I have preached hundreds of sermons, written hundreds of articles, and penned several books. At times people will shed a tear and other times they'll giggle when I share something. Rarely does what I communicate elicit neither response.

If we believe we should live a stoic life with no laughter, we miss the fruit of the Spirit, which is joy. Joy is rarely seen in someone who cannot laugh. Conversely, anyone who cannot be somber at the appropriate time misses the scriptural directive to weep with those who weep.

The challenge is to live in balance. When you experience sadness or euphoria, it's advisable to find perspective. As bad as things might be, trouble is only temporary. Additionally, when things are wonderful, we must temper ourselves with the realization that trouble will come. Doing so will steady us for the inevitable difficulties we face.

I was once told that things are rarely as bad as we think and rarely as good as we think. The key for us all is to keep a balanced view of trouble, pain, victory, and joy. This balance is found in none other than our Lord and Savior Jesus Christ.

A close friend, one I introduced you to earlier, told me one day that he'd decided he didn't want to learn new technologies. So although he can use a computer, he doesn't. He's not that old. His reason? He'll tell you that he has little interest and doesn't want to have to learn how to tweet, post, Skype, and the like. This certainly is his choice, but it got me thinking about how many times people choose to stay ignorant. Some choices aren't important to life and health, but some are. I watch television but have no idea how it works; more than that, I have no desire to find out. The same holds true for my car. I'm truly glad for people who know how my car works, but it doesn't cause me to want to read and educate myself so that I can repair it.

Volitional ignorance is a part of everyone's life, but there's one thing none of us can afford to be ignorant of—and that is life itself.

First, we should be sure to define what life is. Life is more than a physical body that can function in the most primitive ways. Life includes that which we cannot see. All people were created with the ability to love or hurt others beyond physical expressions.

Have you ever heard someone say, "They're dead to me"? Do you have a broken relationship that seems impossible to mend? Have you ever said that something sucked the life out of you? We're talking about more than just "quality of life."

Man has made the horrible choice repeatedly to believe the lie that they know what life is all about. The created cannot arrogantly make decisions regarding life, and yet we do. We've all told the creator that we know better. We have acted like we know what real life is, but the creator alone knows what life really is.

The greatest tragedy in this world is that countless people have believed the lie that life is only related to the physical realm. God told the first human that on the day he disobeyed, he would die (Genesis 2:17). Adam didn't physically die, but his relationship with the creator was broken by this choice.

The story doesn't end there. God went to extraordinary lengths to show all humanity that life is more than a body. Life is relationship with the creator. Sadly, many remain in volitional ignorance of this fact and the remedy.

The "Big T" is on the wall behind me in this photo.

One day, a young boy came to Abundant Life Church. He peered into the sanctuary and saw the beautiful cross on the wall. His words reverberate in my ears even now.

"What is the big T on the wall for?" he asked.

He had no idea of Jesus Christ who came to repair the breach between man and God. We were excited about sharing Jesus with him, but also saddened by his ignorance. He had no parent to teach him of the love of God.

Every week, people drive by churches that have the good news, the gospel of life! Jesus is the life. He is the one who can give life. I've seen many who responded to the message of life, but I've also known some who are content to live in volitional ignorance. One friend told me, "I don't want to know." He's content to clean his hair, eat food, sleep, and clothe himself, but he has chosen to reject life beyond his body. I pray for him and love him anyway. My hope and prayer is that someday he will ask me to tell him about Jesus, the lifegiver. That will be the moment he really has life.

The thief on the cross was about to die, but he chose to not be ignorant of life and said to Jesus, *"Jesus, remember me when You come in Your kingdom!"* (Luke 23:42). He knew two wonderful truths. First, he knew that there was more to life than what he had experienced. Second, he believed that Jesus could do something that would transcend the physical.

Imagine the faith and belief this thief had in Jesus. He was looking at someone who was nailed to a cross and about to die, yet he chose to put his faith and trust in Jesus. Amazing. Although he had lived his life on earth as a criminal, he ended it not in volitional ignorance. My prayer is that you will seek God and reject volitional ignorance.

Don't be surprised when you experience laughter and tears as you read scripture and pray. Frequently, I have. God will speak to you and you will have such joy that laughter will burst from your belly. You'll also shed tears as the Holy Spirit brings conviction and peace to your soul. Nothing is more important than for us to study what God has said in his word and to pray.

The apostle Paul had a lot to say regarding peace, contentment, and joy, especially to the Philippian church, which faced many disturbances. The book of Philippians is a great place to meditate on the value of laughter and tears.

It's my hope that as you've read this book, you will have noticed opportunities to laugh and weep. Please resist avoiding these very real expressions of the human soul. Your life will be fuller and richer because you have laughed and wept.

Remember, my friends, life is all always full of another laugh and another tear. The most important person to share your tears and laughter with is Jesus Christ. Even now, simply surrender your life to him. Then you will be able to gloriously say, "And so the story continues."

As for us, the story does go on. Not long before the publication of this book, Jeremy was married to a wonderful girl, Steph Scott. Now Carole and I are grandparents to the cutest boys, Jackson and Eli. And so the story continues.

MAKING THE CONNECTION

It is a sad fact that most people who do not believe in God have either an incomplete or false understanding of who the Almighty God is. This book, while valuable for such people, is not intended to be an apologetic, nor a defence. Simply, between the covers of this book is one man's observations of God, who has made himself known.

It's more than eternal life that is at stake. It's fellowship with God. Life without the creator is empty; plastic and worthless. It has no meaning. Fellowship with God is more than knowing facts about God. It is life based on who God is. When anyone has relationship with God, they truly live.

ISBN: 978-1-4866-0488-3 • Retail Price: $12.99

CHRISTMAS UNWRAPPED

Christmas comes around every December, followed by the celebration of a New Year. We recycle the same songs. We cook and eat turkey. But what *is* Christmas? To answer that question, we would be wise to turn to the one who brought the event into being. The one who is the subject of this book actually walked the dusty roads of the Middle East. Since his birth, he has impacted lives like no other. He has had more followers than anyone in history. He has been hated by many, and misunderstood by countless more, yet his teaching powerfully influences even the lives of those who don't know him. His name is Jesus.

ISBN: 978-1-4866-1322-9 • Retail Price: $12.99

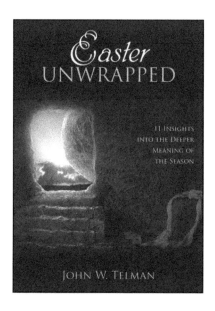

EASTER UNWRAPPED

Life is so much more than merely the physical. You are more than a body. When life hits you between the eyes, when you feel the darkness of death around you, when you're faced with trouble that drains the life out of you, remember Resurrection Sunday. *Easter Unwrapped* presents eleven insights into just how significant the resurrection of Jesus is to everyone. Easter is the day that changed everything, and it's more than chocolate and bunny rabbits. It's about life.

ISBN: 978-1-4866-1243-7 • Retail Price: $11.99